Mommy To Mimi
For Moms of Littles and not-so Littles!

By Mo Mydlo

Acknowledgments

I'd like to first thank you, Justine Bessette for editing this book. Once again, you came to my rescue in the ministry. Your name will always mean, "Just-ine-case we were going to quit, God sent us Justine." Love you girl.

I want to thank you Lesa Schwartz for once again, creating the most beautiful cover design for this book. You are one of the most multi-talented women I know, and I love you dearly.

Thank you to my handsome husband Tommy for loving me through this latest season of life. What a whirlwind growing older can be. I am grateful beyond words God gave me you as my partner on the dancefloor of life. You own my heart and soul forever.

I need to acknowledge my adult kids (yes, they are adults, but they still feel like my babies in my heart). Jake, Travis, Sara and Eli, I am and always will be obsessed with all of you. You are my greatest treasures in life. I thank God for you.
I don't want to forget my daughters –in- law and my son-in-law. Brooke, Darcie and Carlon. You are the answer to my daily prayers I prayed for my kids, for years. God handpicked you beautifully for

each of them. I am beyond grateful for His choices.

I want to acknowledge the staff, board members and volunteers of Unforsaken Women Corporation. You all shine for Jesus. Thank you for inspiring and encouraging me to love God and love people more and more each day.

Dedication

I would like to dedicate this book to my grandchildren. I won't write their names, as those names are tattooed permanently on my heart. I won't tell you the number of grandchildren I have, as I pray that number continues to grow. I won't tell you their ages, as I pray this book blesses mommies for years to come, and that would just not make sense.

I will tell you, I am over the moon, in love with every one of them. I will tell you that their smiles light up the room. I will tell you what I always tell them; "Mimi will always love you. I will always protect you. I will always be there for you. Till I go be with Jesus."

Mommy To Mimi

Yesterday was not a good day for me. My sisters and I had purchased tickets to Cirque de Soliel, and we had plans to celebrate my sister Char's birthday together. Without getting too graphic, let's just say, perimenopause kept me from going. Can I get a middle-aged witness? The good news is, I was able to bless my niece with my ticket. It turned out to be a nice, late birthday present for her.

I am sure I had a cyst burst during church as I was up at the altar as a prayer partner, believing and praying with someone for healing for her husband. You just gotta love God's sense of humor, right? It was Hot-Mess Mo's turn to pray at the altar and I probably could have used some anointing oil myself.

Truthfully, I think God loves to teach us perspective when we are feeling sorry for ourselves in our own misery. The Word says, "Every heart knows its own bitterness." We all have struggles. We all have bad days. We all have leave the altar, and walk quickly to the bathroom after church days. Well, at least I can speak for my perimenopause sisters.

I think God wanted to sit me down again. The truth is, if you know me, you know I don't sit well. I work, I sweat, I push, I serve. Those are my natural tendencies. Sitting for more than one half hour at a time doing anything, even if it is productive like editing, causes me frustration. I wish I could tally up and count the times I have received texts from loving friends of mine that say, "Just rest today Momo" or "God put you on my heart, are you feeling better?" Or "Praying for God to restore you." It's almost embarrassing how badly I am failing the resting in Him test.

I am not good at math. I'm the first to admit that. I joke and say to people, "I don't do math in public." I don't run the register at our thrift store that supports our ministry. It wouldn't be fair on my manager to try and figure out why Mo can't seem to count back the change correctly. I stick to what I know, sorting clothes, setting up displays and loving on customers and praying with food pantry recipients.

I know my gifts and I know my weaknesses. Resting is a weakness for me. So, God sometimes has to put me on my butt to heal from something, so I'll write what He's given me to write, or teach what He's given me to teach. Writing and teaching are my calling. Math and resting are my nemesis.

Now that we have gotten more acquainted, I will share why I'm writing this book. I love encouraging moms. Ministering to mothers is my favorite thing to do because being a mother is my other favorite thing to do. I have loved being a mother since God placed my first son in my womb. I loved being a mom of babies. I loved being a mom of toddlers. I loved being a mom of school aged kids. I loved being a teenager's mom. Today, when my second son who is a father of two, texted me to see how I am feeling I thought, motherhood is my jam. I love it more than anything. Well, almost as much as I love being a Mimi.

Now, I am fixing to preach. That's country girl lingo for "lean your ear in, I have a lot to say about this". I LOVE BEING A MIMI. People tell you all the time how wonderful grandparenting is, and you sort of hear them. But, once you become a grandparent, you completely understand what they are talking about.

My grandparent call sign is Mimi. Why? I won't lie to you; I picked it because it's cute. It sounds very southern and sweet tea, country music and corn bread like. I thought, well, my nieces and nephews call me Momo, so Mimi sounds close to that but it's also special for my grands.

Make no mistake about it, I want my grands to feel special. I want them to feel honored, adored, cared for, loved and protected. I want my grands to receive all the spiritual blessings God has for them. I want my grands to know who they are in Christ at a very young age. I want them to never struggle with insecurity or guilt or shame. I truthfully want them to never experience pain of any kind, ever, in their lives. I only want good for them, and that's gospel truth right there. Do I know this is unrealistic? Of course. But, if you ask me what I want for my kids and grands, I will tell you, I want blessing upon blessing upon more blessing for them. It's the mom in me. It's the Mimi in me.

The truth is, being a wife and mother and now Mimi is my greatest obsession in life after following Jesus. Jesus always gets top billing in my life. After all, I would stink as a wife, mother and Mimi without Him. Holy Spirit Who lives inside of me, because of my relationship with Jesus, drives me. Holy Spirit empowers me to love correctly. Holy Spirit teaches me how to love correctly. Holy Spirit enables me to love correctly. Anything good in me is from Him. I give God the glory for everything, even the love I have for my tribe.

Almost six years ago when my daughter-in-law Brooke and my son Travis told me they were going to have a baby, I was instantly in love with that baby. I didn't know if it was going to be a girl or a boy. That mattered very little to me. It simply mattered that the baby was going to be my grandbaby. He represented the beginning of the next generation of humans endowed with me to love in some way, shape or form. Becoming a Mimi was to be my next adventure to experience with God. I knew I needed Jesus to do it well, just like every other blessing in my life.

How about you? I will testify that I need Jesus so I can be kind. I need Jesus so I can be loving no matter what. I need Jesus so I can treat people well. I need Jesus so I can be patient. (Oh Lord Jesus how I need you for patience.) Sorry for that side prayer. That may happen occasionally during this book.

I need Jesus to help me forgive. I need Jesus to help me stay pure. I need Jesus to help me do pretty much everything, including breath if you think about it. God keeps our heart beating, and He holds our entire lives in His hands. So, you could say, I'm the Jesus girl. He owns all my heart and because of that, He has allowed me to designate a huge part of my heart to belong to The Mydlos and The Holders. My daughter married a Holder, and it took me a long time to stop calling her Sara Mydlo by the way.

Jesus has blessed me with almost 32 amazing years as a mommy and now almost six years as a Mimi. Many great grandparents that are reading this are probably thinking, "*Rookie!*" I admit it, I still have so much to learn about living and loving as a wife, mother and Mimi. I just thought I would share a little of what God has shown me so far. I pray that as I do that, God can add His supernatural strength to it and multiply my efforts, so you are blessed and helped by it in some way, shape or form.

I always try to be helpful in my writing. I'm not that creative to write fiction. I have only written non-fiction so far as a writer. My underlining theme is always, "*Here's some good stories because I'm a hot mess too far from Jesus and He seems to still love me, so I hope this helps you a little.*"

I do not pretend to be great at anything. I truthfully struggle a lot. I struggle with anxiety and insecurity more than I would like to admit. The light at the end of my struggle tunnel has always been renewing my mind in God's beautiful Word and allowing Holy Spirit to guide me and teach me.

I love the motto, know better, do better. When we allow The Word of God to teach us the right things to do and not the wrong, and when we renew our minds to that and align our lives with the Word, we able to do better and I think, help others do better.

My goal for this book is to encourage moms of all ages to love your tribe well. I had a shirt that said, *"Find your people, and love them well."* I loved that shirt as it made me think of my husband and my kids, and my grands, and how blessed I feel to love them well.

Here's a side note, I don't know what happened to that tee shirt. I guess this brings up another one of my weaknesses, laundry. When we were first married my husband asked me if I lacked a laundry enzyme. I don't think that's how it works. But, if there is a reason at a cellular level, I would venture to guess I am laundry enzyme deficient.

I don't separate lights and darks. So, if you leave a white tee shirt at my house, be prepared to come back to pick up a slightly grayish, white one. Sorry, I'm not going to pretend I have Woolite on hand for all your delicates. We own a farm, and the laundry gets cleaned quickly after chores. Clean is the goal, not fancy.

I guess you can see I won't be giving out laundry tips. I do love housework, as it keeps me moving, and I love a clean house, but I will only mention it if there is a spiritual lesson I learned as I cleaned.

I love gardening. That will probably be mentioned. I probably should preface that I couldn't keep a houseplant alive while I had kids living at the house. My goal was to keep kids alive, not rhododendrons. Gardening became a passion of mine after most of my kids grew up.

I love farming, but to be honest, God has had to remind me that I am not a farmer. I am a writer who has a farm. There is a big difference between the two things. Farmers provide food for large groups of people. Writers who have a farm write cute blogs and posts about the silly things their border collie and pigs do daily.

My husband and I milk one goat, one cow and provide our kids with all the farm, fresh eggs they can remember to grab when they visit after church. I bake my own bread, but I don't bake enough sourdough to sell at a bazaar. I bake enough to eat with my peanut butter toast and coffee and raw milk in the morning. I hang my sheets out on the line when I wash them because I like the smell of freshly dried sheets outdoors. But, when it's allergy season, you had better believe the dryer works just fine as well. I mean, why sneeze all night. I think you get me. I'm country, but I am not Laura Ingalls.

So, I'll probably share some cute grandbabies on the farm stories to encourage you. I'll probably share a few garden analogies God has given me to remind us that Jesus is The Vine, and we are the branches, and we need to abide in Him if we want to bear fruit.

I'll probably share a lot of my mistakes. I throw myself under the spiritual bus a lot to help you not make the same mistakes I've made. I don't pretend to have it all together. I only want to point you to the only One Who does, Jesus. I love how John the Baptist said, "I must become less, He must become more." Only as I have become less as a woman, wife, mother and now Mimi and allowed Jesus to reign in me more, have I had anything worthwhile to share.

Friend, I hope you enjoy this journey with me. The trek from Mommy to Mimi has been one of the most rewarding times of my life. May we continue to learn and grow together as we celebrate womanhood in all its glory. The way God designed it to be, ridden with love and laughter, trials and triumphs, sorrows and sadness, and saturated in His goodness and grace.

Best Job in The World

If you ask people what their life's work is, they may tell you, it's the thesis they wrote which made them a doctor, or the business they built from the ground up or the books they have written or movies they have starred in.

If you ask me, what is my life's work. I would tell you; it's my family. It's been the joy of my life being a wife and mother and Mimi. It's been the hardest job I've ever done, and it's been the most enjoyable job I've ever done. Being a mother especially, is what I would consider to be the best Job in the World.

No matter if you are a married mama, a single mama or a widow. You are a working mama whether you bring home a paycheck or not. You simply may work outside the paid labor force as a stay-at-home mom. Though I always used to say to my kids, very rarely do stay at home moms, stay home. Can I get an amen?

We mamas are busy. Our to-do lists could put highly paid executives to shame. If you are a mama who is a highly paid executive, you add that title on top of your already exhausting expectations, it can make you want to run through the drive through for another shot of caffeine in your coffee.

Let's just pause right here as I make a salute to whoever invented coffee. Can we give that genius a round of applause? Seriously, coffee isn't a new thing, I watch Little House on the Prairie and The Waltons and they are sipping that java at all hours of the day and night just to keep up with the chores. I believe coffee is one of those precious gifts from God. I'm pretty sure there will be coffee in Heaven. Yes, Mamas are hard workers. God knew Mama's needed to be tough.

I read this pin one day on Pinterest. Don't even get me started about how fun Pinterest is. It's your one stop shop for sourdough bread recipes, cute outfit ideas, and creative things to do with that old dresser you found in your neighbor's trash on the road.

This pin was amazing. *"The human body can only handle 45 units of pain, but at the time of childbirth a woman endures 57 units of pain which equals 20 fractures at the same time. Never tell a woman she can't do it. Remember, she alone could dance with two hearts and breath with four lungs. Only she could carry the weight of two worlds in her stomach and give birth to life. Don't tell her she's not capable, she's capable of anything."* That's you Mama. Whether you gave birth to your babies or adopted them, this is the type of human God created when He decided to make a mother.

Yes, being a mother is the best job in the world. Whether you feel it right now, or not. You are changing the world.

There's not a job on this Earth of more importance. When God bestows the title of mother on someone, He expects that we will do our utmost to do this job with diligence. With any job, there is usually training. Well, there really isn't a mothering 101 course to take in college, but there is a manual on how to succeed in everyday life, and that is the Bible.

The Word of God has been my lifeline as a wife, mother, and woman of God. Matthew 6:33 says, *"But seek first His Kingdom and His righteousness and all these things will be given to you as well."* I took this scripture literally when I became a Christian and I never turned back from it. I decided I would seek God first every day and I would trust Him to work out the details of that day. And I've never stopped doing this.

I get up before anyone else in the house, and I don't set an alarm anymore, my internal clock takes care of that now, but I get up, I stumble to the coffee pot, I grab my Bible, and I get with Jesus. This is hard to do when babies are little, I know, especially when your babies are nursing all night. But I have found that my quiet time alone with Jesus, is worth every bit of energy it takes to drag yourself out from under those blankets. No matter how hard the night was. Joy truly comes in the morning.

Those first few minutes of the day with Jesus have always been where I thank Him for all my blessings, and those blessings usually start with my husband and kids and our home and our health.

Those first few minutes of the day are when I repent for what I didn't do great the day before, whether in my thinking or my actions, I give my junk and guilt to Him, and He gives me His forgiveness and His ideas on how to be better.

Those first few minutes of the day are when I read some encouraging devotions, some Psalms and Proverbs or work on a Bible study. Those first few minutes are when I equip my mind for action for the rest of the day, by planting God's Word in my heart, so I can use it throughout the day to fight my flesh, the world and the devil. I love 2 Timothy 3:16-17 that reads, *All Scripture is God-breathed and is useful for teaching, rebuking, correcting and training in righteousness, so that the servant of God may be thoroughly equipped for every good work.*

Those first few minutes of the day are when I write down any to-do's that I want to get accomplished each day. Even if those to-dos are my normal everyday chores. If you want to feel accomplished, write out everything you can think of that you do without even thinking each day.

Make coffee
Quiet time with God
Make beds
Make breakfast for family
Get older kids off to school
Make sure kids brush teeth
Take a shower
Put gas in the car before car rider

Let me tell you, if you do this, and you put it on the counter and check it off as each task gets done, by the end of the day at dinner when your husband sees what you actually do during the day, just doing what you have to do to care for your family and the home, he will be shocked at your diligence and you may be shocked as well.

You will see that you really are doing a good job as a housewife and mother. You aren't just surviving until you put on PBS and let Elmo babysit for a few minutes while you shower. You will realize as well you aren't simply surviving until you can get your next Target and Starbucks run in. You are accomplishing a lot. You're managing a family.

Oh, and make sure you do write that one note reminding you when the car needs gas before your kid's car-rider line at school. I'll never forget the time I had to call my sister to rescue me as I was holding up the car-rider line, out of gas and in my purple silk pajamas. When she pulled up, she was dying, laughing at me. It was horrifying at the time, but, well worth the memory now.

Friend, your quiet time with God is crucial. Seek Him first. I know it's hard to carve out the time, but I promise the rewards are worth it. Put your phone away for a few minutes and pick up your Bible. It's way smarter than any smart phone.

Our making a relationship with Jesus, our quiet time with God, and making being in God's Word a priority isn't only for us. It is what we need to teach our kids. I literally love the scripture that says, "I have no greater joy than to hear that my children walk in truth." There is nothing more important to me than knowing my kids know Jesus.

My daughter Sara, who is a mother of two under two, put a little picture on her Instagram story the other day, that blessed my heart. It was her, reading her Bible with my little 1 year old grandson, standing right over the Bible, smiling. I think her post said something like *My Devotions Buddy.* It blessed me so.

That morning, she probably didn't memorize the third chapter of Deuteronomy. She may have only been able to ingest a devotion or a couple of words in red from Jesus that she could take into her day. But what really was gained is, her two babies saw Mommy walking in truth. They are learning by watching Mommy make the Word of God a priority and learning that Jesus is important to Mommy. I pray with every fiber of my being that He will be important to them as well.

I remember a time when Sara was two or three years old, and my friend Mary would come over to do Bible study with me once a week in the evening. My husband was just going to watch the kids in the other room, while we studied.

Well, Mary could never resist Sara saying over and over in her two-year-old little lingo, *"I do "Bi ba" study with you."* I would say *"Sar, go in with Daddy."* Then Mar would say, *"Aww, let her stay."* She would sit on Mar's lap or mine and color while we studied. I look back now and think, Sara was learning that Bible study is important.

The Word says, *Train up a child in the way that they will go and when they are old, they will not turn from it.* Teaching our children about Jesus is the most important lesson we can teach them.

Let me talk about this for a second. I am a list person. I always have been. I am a goal setter. I have a type A personality. I know how us Type A mamas can be. If you know this describes you, lean your ear in.

I remember having mental lists of things I needed to teach my kids. I felt it was my responsibility as a mom.

Things like:

- Make sure they are eating with a spoon and fork, by 13 months.
- Make sure they are saying Mama and Dada and Baby and Baba, by 7 months.
- Make sure they know every nursery rhyme in the mother goose book by 3 years old.
- Make sure they are potty trained by 2 ½.
- Make sure they can ride a bike without training wheels by 5 years old.
- Make sure they can tie their shoes by 5 years old.
- Make sure they play outside at least one hour each day.
- Make sure they eat 3 fruits a day.

Seriously, I had my own check lists, and I was serious about them. It was like my own motherhood report card I gave myself. I really thought all these checklists were my job as a mom to accomplish and some of them are good, but some were a little militant on myself. When the truth is, all that truly matters to me now is that my kids love Jesus and are teaching their kids to love Jesus.

I tell moms now when I speak at events, give them the pacifier. Give them the bottle. If they love it, let it go and let them enjoy these things. I promise they won't take them to college. (If they do, then maybe go talk to someone.) Just kidding.

My kids are all grown now and I praise God that all four of them came to know Jesus as Lord, were baptized, and the married ones have Godly spouses. I pray daily for the same result for our youngest. That's truly the best gift any mother could ask for.

I truthfully am proud of how my grown sons love their wives, support their families financially, love their kids, and take care of their homes, but nothing makes me more thankful than seeing them honor God with their lives.

I have always told them as they got to the age of trying to figure out what careers they may pursue, to not chase money, but do what your heart's desire is, just keep Jesus number one, and you'll be successful. Seek first the Kingdom and His

Righteousness and all these things will be added to you.

Somehow, I knew in my heart of hearts that if I could just keep Jesus as top priority in my life, and in my husband's life, He would be a priority to my kids. The truth is, when your kids grow up knowing God, your job as a mother is easier. You have Holy Spirit to rely on for you and for them. When Holy Spirit is alive in them, He takes His job very seriously. God takes full responsibility for a heart sold out for Him.

I'll never forget when my youngest son Eli was about 14 years old. Each year at Christmas time we would watch the movie *The Nativity* as a family to remember why we are truly celebrating the whole season. We would pop popcorn and sit around the TV together. It has always been one of my favorite Christmas traditions.

At this point, all the older kids had moved out and it was Tommy, me and Eli. One night I said, *"Eli, let's watch the Nativity tonight, it's almost Christmas and we haven't watched it."*
Eli didn't want to. He just wanted to play video games in his room with friends. I started to get sad. I turned to Tommy and asked, *"Why doesn't he want to watch it?"* Tommy said to me, *"Don't worry about it, it's not a big deal."* I felt Holy Spirit

say to me, *"Mo, let it go."* So, I did. I grabbed the movie, and Tommy and I sat down to watch it together.

It was about 5 mins into the movie, and I heard Eli come around the corner into the hallway, toward the kitchen and then the living room. I heard him slowly walk in. He started asking rhetorical questions that He already knew the answers to but wanted me to know he was there. He first asked, *"Is that King Herod?"* I said *"Yes"*.

The next thing I knew, my *"E"* (which is what I normally call him), is sitting right between Tommy and Me. Tommy looked at me and grinned. Holy Spirit inside of Eli, convicted him. I didn't. I didn't guilt him. I didn't make him feel bad for not watching. I just let God be God and I placed my trust in the fact that God lives in Eli and He will grow him up. It's just my job to come alongside God. When the Holy Spirit is in your children, your job becomes a little easier. They have that still small voice guiding them into all righteousness and purity.

Do you know that God loves your children even more than you do? He truly does. Those four children of mine aren't mine. They are God's. I am simply contracted as manager and steward of this home and family, with the mission being, point them Heavenward their whole life.

Truthfully, nothing really matters but eternity. Will your family be with you in Heaven someday? We must think about that when we are weighing our priorities in life.

 I've been in the ministry for many years. I led groups called *MOPS (Mothers of Preschoolers).* I've done construction ministry. I've done outreach ministry. Now I am a writer and teacher of women and children. But I truly believe that if I don't keep my priorities in order of Jesus first, my husband second, and my children and grandchildren third, then my ministry fourth, God won't bless it. If I go out trying to save the world and my family falls apart, what good is it?

Mama, your most important disciples share a roof with you, or they once did. Personally, I am now 100% positive that my grandchildren are my most important disciples that I am responsible for now.

It is imperative to me that they all know that Mimi loves Jesus, and she loves them, but more importantly, Jesus loves them. I say to them every time I see them or rock them, *"Mimi will always love you. I will always protect you. I will always be there for you. Till I go be with Jesus."*

I love singing *Jesus Loves Me* to the babies and *Jesus Loves the Little Children.* I let them watch *The Donut Man*, which is an old silly 80's Christian show while they jump on the couch and sing in my living room. We have a game we like to play; we call it *Pond Pond*. I played it with my kids and now I play it with their kids. They take all of the cushions off the couch and all the blankets and pillows, and I let them jump into the pond and dance. It helps them get a lot of energy out, especially if it's raining out, or just hot out and we've already played outside.

Mama, you have the most amazing job. Being a mom is the best job in the world, but do you know, it doesn't have to be as complicated and expensive as we've made it? Kids do not want anything except your time.

There's a lot of pressure out there on moms to stay up on the latest trends in mothering, especially because of social media and its pressures. Influencers are getting paid big bucks to tell you what you should and need to buy and have, what the newest techniques are, and what is *"trending."*

Mom, can I minister to you for a second? I need to tell you the truth. All your babies need, is you, and when I say babies, I mean babies of all ages. They need you, Mom. God knew that when He gave you breasts which produces all their food for the first year of life. He made your babies and kids need their mommy close.

Eli is 20 now. On his 19ᵗʰ birthday we went out to lunch. We went to a sub shop. A mom was sitting across from her school aged daughter. She had obviously just picked her up from school as she had a school uniform on. The girl was telling mom all about her day, and mom was on her phone. The little girl was talking to mom's forehead the whole time as mom's eyes were on her phone, not her daughter. The little girl just kept talking. I saw Eli look at them. I said to Eli, *"You want that mom to put her phone down, don't you?"* He said, *"Mom, she just wants her mom to listen."* It was so obvious to both of us. Kids do not need much. They need you, mom.

My Daughter is a mommy, and she still needs me, differently, but still, she needs me, and I need her. Same with my grown sons. They are fathers but they still need my husband and me.

God has given us everything we need to enjoy our kids as we raise them. God gave us sunshine, to take our kids outside and play so they fill up on Vitamin D naturally to stay healthy. God has given us water, to fill their little sippy cups with, so they stay hydrated when they play and so they poop good. (Sorry, this author loves talking about poop.) Make sure you drink a lot of water my friend, pooping is important.

God has given us grass, to walk on barefoot so our kids can get the health of the ground through their bodies and stay healthy. God has given us the ocean and local lakes and parks to visit, with a bag of sand toys, some peanut butter and jelly sandwiches and some sunscreen for a full morning outside. And you had better believe those babies will sleep well that night after a day at the beach or the park.

God has given us animals to care for and teach the kids the importance of caring for others and the unconditional love that animals can give us. God has given us rain to play in with rain boots and umbrellas, and mud to make mudpies with. God has given us hoses to make waterslides with our backyard slide on the swing set and a baby pool. Not everyone has a pool. The water hose is more fun anyways.

God has given us flour and water and salt to make homemade Play doh with the kids. God has given us blankets to build forts in the living room with, tying blankets to chairs with clothespins and eating snacks in the fort together as you talk about their favorite things. Kids want to talk about their favorite cookies, favorite songs, favorite foods, you name it, kids love talking about their favorite things.

God has given us an imagination to use and to remember what it was like being a kid, playing school, and office and house and library. These are the things I played with my kids, and now these are the things I play with my grandbabies. They help me remember that life is fun when you don't take it so seriously.

Part of excelling at the best Job in the world, being a mom, is remembering how to play. Play is how kids learn. It is how kids express emotions. It's how kids tire themselves out, so they eat and sleep well. My grown kids still love when we have a family kickball game, or throw the football around in the yard, or play a fun board game together when they visit. It is quality time, and you can't get that from a computer or phone or device.

Being a mom is the best job in the world. As you play with them, you can teach them. I was painting with my grands one day on the porch at their little play table and I said, *Mimi is going to teach you the ten commandments today.*

Well, as I was teaching them, Jackson, who at the

time was a hilarious 4-year-old (he's still pretty hilarious by the way) turned to me and said, *"Mimi, I lie sometimes."* I said, *"I know honey, we all break the commandments sometimes, that's why we ask Jesus for His forgiveness, and we start again."* He then said, *"Yes, I do that, but I lie again."* I giggled by accident and said, *"We sure need Jesus don't we, my love?"* I love that boy; He doesn't even realize just how honest his little heart is.

We have a lot to learn from kids just like they have a lot to learn from us. My kids and grands have taught me more about faith, then any amount of church and Bible study can. We must watch how kids believe, and we need to be like them.

Matthew 5:1-5 reads: *At that time the disciples came to Jesus and asked, "Who, then, is the greatest in the kingdom of heaven?" He called a little child to him and placed the child among them. And he said: "Truly I tell you, unless you change and become like little children, you will never enter the kingdom of heaven. Therefore, whoever takes the lowly position of this child is the greatest in the kingdom of heaven. And whoever welcomes one such child in my name welcomes me.*

Do you not think the faith of a child is important? Don't think your ministry at home with your kids is important? Don't think God calls it important? The scriptures tell us just the opposite. They are the most important disciples you will ever have, share a roof with, or once shared a roof with.

We have so much to learn from our kids about faith. I can't tell you how many times my kids have turned around and preached something to me that I have preached to them. They are listening, my friend. They are soaking it all in.

If you want to know what you look like, watch your kids play. They emulate you. Little girls act just like mommy when they are mothering their dolls. Little boys act like daddy when they are playing with their action figures. We need to set an example for them in faith, as we also let them show us how to have the faith of a child. What is done for eternity matters. The things of this Earth will one day pass, only what's done for the Kingdom will last.

My mama passed away on August 9th of last year. She struggled with Rheumatoid arthritis for 30 years, and Jesus brought her home, so that she would have no more pain, no more struggles, no more flare ups, no more tears.

My mama was brilliant, she was the valedictorian of her graduating class. She could have gone to any college and pursued any career, but she used to say, *"All I ever wanted to be, was a mom."*

My mom had 7 kids and more grands and great grands than I can count. Let's just say my mom filled 83 stockings every Christmas, and this is just family.

The day my mama collapsed in my Daddy's arms, he called the ambulance and within minutes me and all my six siblings met them in the emergency room. My mom told us at the hospital,*" I am dying."* Her vitals backed her up. The hospital broke a few rules and allowed us all to be in the room with her at once. The rule was 2 at a time, but they knew our time was limited. So, my Daddy and all of us kids were at her bedside, then slowly, all our kids showed up, and some of their kids. As my mama was struggling in pain, we watched God do a beautiful miracle, in the ER of our hospital, grandchild, by grandchild kept coming.

Every one of my mom's kids and grands who lived in Florida at the time made it to my mom's bedside and she addressed them all by name. She even knew them when her eyes were closed. She knew their voices. Though she was the one leaving, she consoled those who were inconsolable.

They all kept telling her how much they loved her and how special she was to each one of them. The nurses in the ER kept saying, *"I've never seen anything like this. I can see Jesus all over your family. It feels like it's my family."*

You see, my mama, fulfilled her mission in life. She wanted to be a mother and God made her a mother, and a grandmother and a great grandmother and she loved her family purposefully.

At her bedside, she kept saying, *"I'm going to be with Jesus."* She told my daddy, *"I'm sorry, but you have to let me go,"* My mama had faith, the faith that Jesus teaches us to have, the faith of a child. She knew exactly where she was going, and she was excited to get there. With this many children and grands, how could she not have the faith of a child?

We knew at my mom's funeral we couldn't do an open microphone in the service, I mean, with the size of this family the pastor would have never been able to go home. So, we opened the mic at the reception afterwards and one by one each family member came up and shared what my mom (Didi which is what the grands called her) meant to them. It lasted hours, and all the guests stayed. They knew they were witnessing something rare. It was a day all of us who were there will never forget.

Yes, I miss my mama dearly, and my daddy misses her more. 58 years of marriage is a long time. But I will see her again, and so will all of us who have made Jesus Lord of our lives. So, we fix our eyes on that.

My mama's legacy reminds me that this message is true; mothering is truly the best job in the world. We may not see financial rewards from it, but the rewards of an amazing legacy living on beyond us, the legacy of a Godly mother, is the most impactful thing you can ever devote your time to.

Mommy,
Love your husband.
Love your babies.
Love your grand babies.
Love your tribe well. Make a difference in eternity by loving your people the way Jesus taught us to love, unconditionally.

A Calm Mind

I want to talk to you about your emotions today. Oh, yes, this one is a fun one, right? I mean, I am pretty daring to write a book for women, especially mothers and grandmothers who may be hormonal, nursing, or pregnant, going through the change of life, and sleep deprived or wondering where all those good hormones went to and saying, "*We are going to get a grip on our emotions.*" It's like going into a shopaholics' anonymous meeting and talking about living on a budget. Not an easy sell.

Friend, I promise, I'm here relating to you as a fellow woman, a perimenopausal woman, truthfully wishing I was a menopausal woman, (I mean, how long can this "peri" thing last? For the love!) but saying, *"Come on sister, we gotta get a grip!* Both of us. Because, let me tell you, I have learned the hard way that losing it emotionally accomplishes nothing, except that the devil has a ball after we have a fit, making us feel guilty for it.

The truth is, we have complete self-control over our emotions, whether we feel it or not. No, I am serious. If you are a Christian woman, which means, you have accepted Jesus Christ as your personal savior, then you have self-control. I know this because the bible teaches that the second you accepted Christ, you were given the fruit of self-control.

Yes, self-control is a fruit of the spirit. Now, whether we choose to walk in that fruit is up to us. Whether we decide to cultivate that fruit is up to us. This goes for all the other fruits of the Spirit. We can walk in love, joy, peace, patience, kindness, goodness, faithfulness and gentleness. We have these fruits. We simply must choose to walk in them.

I promise you; I sometimes have to self-talk myself The Word of God in my everyday life to avoid having an emotional fit about the littlest things because I am in perimenopause. Here we are again, perimenopause talk. Well, I opened the can of worms, let's dig in.

What does Peri mean anyways? I think it means, *"Buckle up sister, this is going to take a while."* I used to have a television show called, *"Moments with Mo"*, Now, I'd like to have one called, *"A Menopause Moment"* I think it would get way better ratings. I mean, the whole unpredictability of menopause could be a reality show.

I saw a diagram of what our hormones do during perimenopause. It's just as unpredictable and up and down as a teen going through puberty is. Now,

I am a mom, and I remember all too well how crazy my kids got during puberty. My husband likes to say, during puberty, boys get dumber, and girls get meaner. I think he's spot on. Thank God our little beautiful humans come back to us after a little while.

Truthfully, because of these hormones I'm dealing with, I must kill my ugly flesh before it has a hay day. We all do. We must renew our minds and crucify our flesh everyday if we want to look like Jesus.

Do you know that we are supposed to start looking like Jesus to the world? We are. If we are supposed to start acting like Jesus, because as believers in Jesus Christ; we carry Christ on the inside of us, we need to see how Jesus kept his cool all the time. What did Jesus do first to keep his cool in crazy situations?

He got quiet with the Father often. Luke 5:16 says; But Jesus often withdrew to lonely places and prayed.

I know what you are thinking:
"Well, praise The Lord Mo, that's easy for you to say; Your youngest is 20. You can easily find a quiet place and get with God and pray. I have one on my

*side, one on my boob, and one in the stroller, I
don't have a lot of alone time right now."*
*Or "I am working full time, caring for my home,
caring for my husband and my kids and now my
oldest daughter just moved back in with her baby
after a difficult divorce with her husband."*
*Or "I am doing my best to keep my cool, but my
husband of 50 years just passed away and I am on
my own just trying to figure out how to get out of
bed some days."*

Sister, I get it. I promise. No matter what stage of
life we are in, as difficult as it may seem, we must
carve out time alone with The Lord, if we want to
maintain our mental stability.

Jesus knew He had to withdraw from the crowds
to pray. Get this my friend, He was God, and if He
needed quiet time to stay in God's will, we most
assuredly do. If we think that we can keep our
cool and stay in perfect peace in the middle of the
storms of life without that quiet time with God
each day, we are wrong. We can only keep up with
the craziness for so long and then we become like
a tee-pot on the stove, that will start whistling as
soon as the heat gets high enough.

Jesus kept his cool because He beat the craziness
of the world throughout His day by getting alone
with the Father, and during those times He gained

strength. We have too as well. It is imperative that we find that alone time. That means we must learn to say no to some of the 8000 invites we get to things. Learning to manage a healthy schedule as a woman, wife and mother and learning that these three words *"No, thank you"* Can help us get a grip on our emotions like never before.

We must learn to get alone and quiet with God if we want victory in our walk as Christian women. Our alone time with God will improve our marriages. Our alone time with God will improve our parenting and grandparenting. Our alone time with God will strengthen our testimonies. It is imperative.

The second thing Jesus did consistently to keep His cool in crazy circumstances is, He had a couple close friends that He could trust.
Peter, James and John were the only disciples that Jesus had with Him at the transfiguration. He had 12 disciples, but Jesus didn't have all 12 of them there with Him all the time, seeing all His business. He had three men He trusted with a few special moments.

The disciple John referred to Himself as *"The disciple whom Jesus loved."* Oh, I'm sure that bugged Peter and James, but truthfully, John knew He was loved by Jesus because Jesus confided in

Him, taught Him, and relied on Him. We all need to gain an understanding of how much we are loved by God. That only comes from time, with Him, alone. When we spend quality time with Jesus, we begin to realize that we are the disciples who Jesus loves too.

Yes, Jesus didn't share everything with all the disciples. At one point Jesus only allowed James, Peter, and John to accompany Him when He went to heal Jairus' daughter, actually, raise her from the dead. Why not all the disciples? I don't know, maybe He knew their lack of faith may impede the miracle.

I wonder if maybe some of your "*friends*" that you are sharing every little detail of your everyday life with on social media are as trustworthy as you think. I know that hurts, but believe me, I'm preaching to myself too.

I've had to learn boundaries. I'm a people- person. I trust people too quickly and not everyone who calls themselves your friend is your friend. They don't always have your best interest at heart. Even if they type a heart on your picture or hit like. Jesus had a few, true friends that He could trust; and He built and cultivated those relationships, and we have too as well. We truthfully only need a few authentic friends that we can confide in, that we can be real with, that when we mess up, will forgive us and likewise. True friendship doesn't come in the thousands like we see on social media. We must cultivate and work to protect true friendships.

True friendships share face-to-face time with each other, not just screen time. We are made for community and in order to be the amazing wives and mothers that we want to be, we need a few close friends that we can trust to encourage us and spur us on in faith.

Jesus got alone with the Father. Jesus had a few trusted friends. And Jesus kept a grip on His emotions by knowing how to submit to authority. Who was Jesus' authority? The Father.

In the Garden of Gethsemane when Jesus knew He was getting ready to be betrayed and was facing His death, He prayed this prayer in submission to The Father. "Father, if thou art willing, remove this cup from me; yet not my will, but thine be done" (*Luke 22:42*). Jesus approaches The Father in submission, almost as if to say, *God I don't want to do this, but because It's your will, I will.*
How good are you at submitting to authority? Because truthfully, I could use some pointers from Jesus. Let's talk about submitting to our husbands. Shall we? I can feel both you and I squirming in our

seats right now. But the truth is, we must be intimate with our husbands on a regular basis. No matter how tired we are. I have had to learn this the hard way in our 33 years of marriage.

I know women are not made the same as men. Why do you think God had to command us to submit to them? Because quite honestly, after making dinner, cleaning up, getting the kids off to bed and finally having some alone time with our hubbies, the last thing we want to do is put on a pretty nightgown and look nice for them. Truthfully, most of the time, I want to put on my 12-year-old flannel monkey jammies and watch a re-run of Seinfeld. Too real?

This is where we must be creative. Because truthfully, I think we are working too hard as women. We are killing ourselves all day long scrubbing grout on the tile, rushing the kids to violin lessons, serving at PTO and church, then trying to make the gourmet meal that we saw on some food network, with ingredients that we have never even had in our houses and this girl on the show somehow grew them out back in her garden. Then, when our husbands come home, we don't understand why he doesn't notice that the kids are on the couch dressed in white, supper is served, and we feel like we have been hit by a truck.

When, truthfully, we could have made macaroni and cheese for dinner and then that night given him sex, and he would brag at work the next day about how amazing his wife is. Sister, most men are simple. They want food (not even fancy food) and sex. That's it. For the most part, if you get those two things right, I'm telling you, your marriage will get better.

Jesus knew how to submit to authority. Our husbands are supposed to be the spiritual leaders of the home, whether they act like it or not. I want to encourage you to submit to your husband as the spiritual authority, until he starts acting like it.

If you are struggling with submission to your husband, pray to God about it in your quiet time. Ask God to help you to submit. God is faithful. He wants to help us in every area of our lives. Our marriages are important to God. We entered a covenant with our spouses before God. God takes that very seriously.

Maybe you can ask a few of your trustworthy friends to help encourage you to be a submissive wife. Good godly friends will be the iron that sharpens iron.

I am grateful for my friend Chrissy who will say tough things to me when she thinks I need to hear it. I'll never forget when Chrissy and her husband Pete went on vacation with Tommy and I to a homestead festival and she pushed me a little about submitting more to Tommy sexually. She encouraged me to step up my effort in this area of our marriage and I considered that to be God speaking through her to me and I took it seriously.

Good friends are hard to come by. We have a lot of social media friends and followers but unless these people are doing day-to-day life with us, we need to consider them more of an acquaintance. True friends are in the trenches with us.

When Tommy heard that Chrissy challenged me in this area, her stock went way up in his eyes. After all, Tommy thinks I should somehow fit it into every message I teach, and every book I write. Yes, I am sure he will like this chapter.

Jesus got alone with the Father often. Jesus had a few trusted friends. Jesus submitted to authority. And Jesus studied the Word and He spoke the Word out loud to fight temptation.

After Jesus was baptized, the first place The Holy Spirit led Him to, was out in the wilderness to be tempted by The Devil. Do you know what three words Jesus used to fight The Devil? It is written. Jesus quoted scripture at Satan to fight him and his temptations. Friend, if you think you can fight the temptations of this world, your flesh, and the enemy and win without The Word. You are wrong.

We need to know the Word. Because we will try other things, and they won't work. They may give you temporary relief, but only The Word applied to our lives causes lasting change of any kind.

Take heart, even pastors and Bible teachers and ministry leaders forget sometimes that The Word is all we need. When we venture out like emotional wrecks into the community or we start typing on the internet when we are feeling emotional or we react in situations emotionally, it doesn't usually end well. Can I get a witness?

 It takes a village to dig us out of the holes we've dug and wow the poor casualties along the way. But if we can remember to just go to The Word. If we can just learn to say; *"No devil! Not today"* Or *"I have a spirit of self-control!"* Or *"I am a child of God. I have the fruit of Spirit. I have everything I need to live a self-controlled and fruitful life."*

If we can speak the Word out loud to ourselves, we can calm ourselves down. Faith comes by hearing and hearing by the Word of God. We must let God's Word go out our mouths and into our ears, so it can penetrate our hearts.

We need to say to ourselves things like:

"I am fearfully and wonderfully made."

"I am the righteousness of God in Christ Jesus."

"I can do all things through Christ who gives me strength."

"As for me and my house we will serve The Lord."

"The Lord is God over my feelings and emotions."

"I can do this! In Jesus Name."

We need to talk ourselves down, so it doesn't take a village to help us back up. We need to do what Jesus did and speak the Word out loud to our tempting emotions. We need to say; *"It is written!"*

We are in total control of these emotions that we have. We can get a grip on them and live peaceful God-fearing lives. We can look like Jesus and not like the hot mess we feel like.

We must get alone with The Father. We must find a few close friends that we can trust and cultivate real relationships with face to face, not over a monitor or screen. We must submit to authorities in our lives. Even though we are adults we still must submit to authority and, we must have the Word ready on our tongues to speak out loud to our tempting emotions. True and lasting peace is available. We can walk in it. We must follow Jesus. He is our peace.

Don't Trust Your Feelings

Coming right out of the shoot I'm going to say, Feelings are a good thing, and God gave them to us for a reason. Ok, so now you can hear me out. Your feelings are real and so are your thoughts and dreams, but they should never be your compass that you determine your direction in life by. You need The Word of God.

Our feelings are still part of our flesh, which takes its cues from our 5 senses. Our feelings change by the millisecond. Here's some proof for you. This morning as I woke, I was heading to my coffee with the song "You Give Good Love" by Whitney Houston running over and over in my mind. It was most likely the last song I heard yesterday. When I sat on my prayer swing to pray and listen for God's voice, this is what went through my mind:

- I thanked God that Eli and Tommy's little sound in their throat was just pollen in the air.
- Then I thought about how much pollen was all over the furniture that I needed to rinse off.
- I looked out at the cows and thanked God for our cow Elsa laying in the field who I pray is pregnant.

- Then I wondered if we should move the cows to the other side of the fence for a little while to help them naturally fertilize more of the grass.
- Then, my mind bounced to bees and pollen and how I was thinking about the poor guy who came into the resale shop yesterday and wanted to enjoy his shopping, but his allergies were driving him crazy.
- I thought he looked like someone I graduated with.
- Then my mind thought about the fact that I was the Class President in high school and that I really need to think about a reunion soon.
- Then my mind started doing math on how long I've been out of school.
- I thought and wondered where we would have the reunion. What would that look like?
- I thought then about how long my kids have been out of school and what reunion they may be going to.
- Then, I thought about every one of my grands and how babysitting went yesterday and that I really needed to drop off those action figures off to the boys.

Are you getting the drift? Our feelings and thoughts are like the longest run on sentence ever. What started out with a plan to pray and be still before God, turned into figuring out, organizing, planning and doing. My thoughts wandered from prayer, to overcoming allergies, regenerative farming, high school reunion planning, to family, and so much more. And this was about 15 minutes.

Our only true North is The Bible. Renewing our minds in The Word keeps us on the path of God's will for our lives. Our feelings change quicker than we can say rest! I recognized my soul was to distracted, so I sat still, and I breathed in and out and said *"Yahweh Saves"* about 4 times. The name of Jesus translates as Yahweh Saves.

Quickly I went inside and stuck my face in The Bible until my thoughts calmed down. We must mind our mind and tell our feelings and thoughts they don't get to choose our direction in life, we do.

We get to choose to line our thoughts and feelings up to The Word and we get to choose to walk in peace. Thank you, Jesus, for this choice. *"My flesh and heart may fail, but God is the strength of my heart and my portion forever."* (Psalm 73:26)

The Secret Place

If we are going to walk in the perfect peace that Christ died for us to walk in, we must learn to abide in The Secret Place of The Most High God. We need a Secret Place to meet with God so that the distractions of the world, the wiles of The Enemy, and the selfishness of our flesh doesn't get the best of us.

Recently we gave a car to a single mother through our ministry. The ministry was blessed with a donated car, and we had a single mother in need, and it worked perfectly for her to receive it. It was a beautiful night. A couple families showed up to her home and surprised her. To say there were some tears shed, some hugs given, and some love tanks filled up, is an understatement. This is the good stuff in ministry. These are the days that you remember why you do what you do daily. These are the days that the blood, sweat and tears shed in hard work each day are all worth it.

I did a public announcement on our ministry social media page to celebrate this win for the Kingdom of God. As a ministry, it's important that our donors and sponsors see the fruit that their giving is creating here as we love people and share Christ with them.

I was tempted to give accolades to the family that donated the car until I felt a nudge in my Spirit to keep that a little quieter. God put Matthew 6:1-4 on my mind, *"Be careful not to practice your righteousness in front of others to be seen by them. If you do, you will have no reward from your Father in heaven.*

"So, when you give to the needy, do not announce it with trumpets, as the hypocrites do in the synagogues and on the streets, to be honored by others. Truly I tell you, they have received their reward in full. But when you give to the needy, do not let your left hand know what your right hand is doing, so that your giving may be in secret. Then your Father, who sees what is done in secret, will reward you."

I love the generous donors of the van too much to steal their eternal rewards from them by covering them with the cheap substitute of what will probably be; three days of hearts and praying hands emojis and a few *"at a boy"* comments here and there on social media, until something else starts to trend.

I want these beautiful friends of ours who donated a safe, reliable van to a mother and two boys in need, to get their deserved crowns in Heaven that is promised to those who do God's work while here on Earth. You see, if they are crowned here, there is no crown there. As a ministry leader, I'm not making that decision for them. That's up to them to decide where their coronation takes place.

I'm convicted about this often as the Director of our ministry. People need to see what the ministry represents and supports to decide if they want to financially partner with us. Therefore, we share on our ministry website and social media platforms, the "wins" for the Kingdom. We share the things that Heaven calls good because let's face it, it takes money to do ministry.

A lot of the time because my face is shown in those pictures, my name is attached to the descriptions, and my signature signs checks, I receive praise from men here on Earth more than I would prefer to admit. The truth is, when I was a spiritual baby, I loved that praise. I ate it up. I needed it to fill my unhealthy people-pleasing void in my heart.

I thrived on the adrenaline rush of people telling me what a "good person" I was. Mainly because my need and desperation for a Savior screamed at me how far from good I was.

Unfortunately, those words of affirmation were like placing band-aids on a hemorrhaging, wounded soul. I only felt good until my next attack of guilt or shame from the enemy took place, and that would hurl me headfirst into overactive serving and performing to please people again and get another fix of praise.

People-pleasing and approval addiction is exhausting and detrimental to our health. It took a good old- fashioned case of burn out to turn this quintessential Martha into a Mary for good. (Luke 10:38-42).

After 6 years of working as the Outreach Director for a once small church that exploded into a mega-church, God rescued me from myself, when He called me to quit my job and begin writing and teaching women. God said to me, *"Help women think right."* Which is quite humorous to me now when I think of how poorly my thought patterns were and are without my daily renewal of my mind by The Word of God.

God was calling me to help women think right as He would teach me to do so as well. Our Unforsaken Women Ministry is 14 years old, and my calling hasn't changed much since then. Here's the pattern. I struggle with my thinking, God straightens me out with His Word, then He says,

"Now share it." I wrote a book called *Overcoming Anxiety, Your Biblical Guide to Breaking Free from Fear and Worry.* You would think that I would be something of an expert at not worrying by now after penning a book with that title, wouldn't you? Nope! I say all the time, *"I'm an overcomer, not an overcamer."*

Part of my healing from anxiety, over-active thinking, insecurity, and people-pleasing (and you thought you were a mess) is that God has said to me, *"Mo, you have to be real so people can heal."* God has called me to be ridiculously and awkwardly transparent to heal and help others heal.

God showed me Hebrews 12:12-13 supernaturally one day. This is a biblical example of why I must work at my healing from fear and anxiety, because my healing is not only for me, but it is also for many others.

"Therefore, strengthen your feeble arms and weak knees. "Make level paths for your feet," so that the lame may not be disabled, but rather healed." I thank God for His grace and mercy as I continue to learn from my Teacher, Holy Spirit, how to walk in freedom in my thinking by daily renewing my mind in the Word of God. I also, thank Him for the absolute privilege of serving others daily in a full-

time ministry, writing and teaching The Word of God.

Matthew 6:3-4 reads, *"But when you give to the needy, do not let your left hand know what your right hand is doing, so that your giving may be in secret. Then your Father, who sees what is done in secret, will reward you."* If our giving is done in secret, we can be confident in knowing that our Father in Heaven is keeping score. He's making mental notes of our altruism, and He is preparing our rewards for us in eternity. I think what excites me the most about this concept is that in doing this kind of giving, it's like we have a private and classified, personal and intimate secret with God. It's like we are besties.

Have you discovered the amazing, and miraculous experience of being close and personal friends with The God of the Universe? Have you declared Jesus as Lord of your life, and given Him the other half of your BFF necklace? Remember those? I never had one special BFF to give the other necklace to at any one time. God always seemed to have two or three close friends take a little piece of my heart at a time.

This left me hanging at Claire's accessory shop in the mall when I wanted so badly to buy those paired necklaces. I always seemed to gravitate to the hoop earrings after. There's something about cute hoops, a tank top, jean shorts or jeans, and flip flops in the summer or cowboy boots in the winter. That look was mine when I had the biceps and hamstrings to pull them off and it's mine now, even though I don't. Thank God for a cute cardigan to cover the bicep mishap I have going on right now.

I quite honestly think the reason God never gave me one best friend at a time, is He knew my clingy heart too much. He knew my inclination to co-depend. He knew how weak and insecure I was and if another girl or guy ever filled that role for me, I would self-destruct in idolatry, and they would have more on their hands than they would know how to handle.

Jesus had reserved BFF for Himself, before He created me in my mother's womb. *"Before I formed you in the womb I knew you, and before you were born, I consecrated you; I appointed you a prophet to the nations."* Jeremiah 1:5. Sometimes when I am having a *"God-fident"* moment (God-fident Translation: "Knowing I can't do it alone, but with God, I can do it.") I sit in awe thinking how thankful I am that God called me to preach and teach. When I say awe, I really mean awe. I can't believe it in the natural that God knew me so intimately before I was ever even attached to my mother's umbilical cord, that He decided I would be a soldier in His army someday.

My mama never told me as a child, she never told me as a teenager and she never told me as a young adult, that she had a supernatural experience with God as a young mom rocking me. She said, God spoke to her and said, *"She will work for me someday."* She did not tell me this until after I had worked a while for Jesus in ministry.

Why did she never tell me? I think, as a mother, we don't want our children following our plans for them, we want them following God's. Something in her probably thought, *"If this is God and not just the postpartum talking, He will call her when He's ready for her"*. She was right.

I've had two similar experiences with my two youngest of my four kids. I'm sure I would have had more if I had been following Him earlier. He was waiting on me. He's so patient with us. Once I could truly decipher His voice, God began talking to me in the Secret Place with Him. He shared things about my kids that I chose not to share with them just in case it would interrupt God's plans for their lives.

The point is, Jesus is my BFF. He's my Heart's Desire, My Healer, My Counselor (Lord have mercy I consistently need a counselor), My Deliverer, My Sustainer, My Mighty Fortress I Run To, My Root I Am Attached To, My Hiding Place, My Husband, My Father, My Peace, My Protector. Do I need to keep going? I am sure I have broken too many English language rules with all my capitals, but there is no way on earth I'll ever talk about my Jesus without a capital letter. He has earned His capital in my book.

Jesus is my Companion at my Secret Place. I have one. Do you? Do you have a place where you and Jesus meet and communicate? I'm not saying that you can't communicate with Him everywhere, every second, every time of the day and night, no matter where you are, no matter what you are doing.

I thank The Lord often that He doesn't mind even travelling with me to the bathroom and God knows some of my most supernatural downloads have been when I am worshipping in the shower.

There's a funny old comedy called The Dream Team. This movie portrayed a rag-tag group of hilarious characters from a mental institution. The best part of the movie was the diversity of the characters. Well, there was one character that walked around naked a lot. One scene he walked into a church. I think there was a wedding going on in the scene. (It's been many years since I've watched movies that showed nudity, so excuse my failure to remember all the details.) But, when he walks in and sees people obviously uncomfortable, he says, *"We're all naked in the eyes of The Lord."* Why I had to share that detail, I don't know, it was just plumb funny. That's all.

Though I speak with Jesus everywhere, all the time, I have a Secret Place that I meet with Jesus daily. It's my porch swing. I have penned the majority of my books and blogs, social media posts and even well thought out texts (with carefully placed emojis) from that swing.

My secret place with Jesus has been drenched in tears, soaked by rain, and even covered in dog hair when my Border Collie is shedding in the hot, Florida, summer months. Her name is Hady, and she loves my prayer swing as much as I do. She isn't allowed on the couch or furniture, but when I hit that swing, she is like, *"Oh heck yes, it's cuddle and prayer time."*

My swing is my secret place. Do I think that swing is anointed? Nope, unless black coffee and peanut butter toast is the magic anointing oil God has used. I don't think it is anointed; I think it was appointed. I think God sat my burnt-out butt in it years ago as if to say, *"Now, sit and rest here while I heal you."*

I specifically set the swing facing East to see the sunrise with God each morning. Now, don't think I'm legalistic, there are many times I miss it when the beauty of perimenopausal hormones interrupt my sleep in the night which causes me to wake a couple minutes past sunrise. But, for the most part God allows me to hear that automatic coffee pot go off, at about the same time the roosters, crickets, donkeys and cows, acres away are waking up to the sun with me. I get a little Maxwell House pep in my step knowing, I am only a couple stretches, a toothbrushing and a walk to let the dog out from our secret time together in the morning.

I get excited about our time together. I get excited about my Secret Place with God. I mean, it's ours. It belongs to me and Jesus alone. Well, Hady too when she's out there with me. That is our time. This is my special meeting with God. This is when Holy Spirit can calm my over-active thinker, re-set my exhausted soul, remind me what is real, and what I had only imagined to be real. He can allow me to lay my guilt and shame at His feet and wait for the supernatural peace that passes all understanding to guard my heart and mind again.

My Secret Place is where I can share my anxious, fretful, worried, sometimes even heinous, and embarrassing thoughts with God and for some reason, He takes them, and He rises to show me compassion. Isaiah 30:18, *Yet the LORD longs to be gracious to you; therefore, he will rise up to show you compassion. For the LORD is a God of justice. Blessed are all who wait for him."*

My Secret Place is where I can ask God to make me a better wife, mother, Mimi, sister, daughter, friend, and ministry leader. I can share with Him my inability to be any of these things on my own without Him. He then shows me; I am never alone.

In the Secret Place, God gave me the name of our ministry, Unforsaken Women. He used the Word to show me that I am never alone, and I will never, ever, be alone again, and I never will be forsaken. He will never leave me or forsake me. I am unforsaken. Joshua 1:5 will always be our ministry's life verse. *"No one will be able to stand against you all the days of your life. As I was with Moses, So I will be with you; I will never leave you nor forsake you.*" God gave me the word Unforsaken. He said, "*You are Unforsaken.*" It's not even a word. It's not in the dictionary. In true grammatical English it would be, "*You are not forsaken.*" Now that's just another thing that I think is so cool about God. He doesn't care if Webster or Merriam call it a word. If God says it's a word, it's a word.

I think He also knows I am just a little too country not to call something a word just because it's not in the dictionary. Half of my verbiage that I use daily is a combination of things my Grandma Eleanor or her mama, my Great Grandma Carr used to say while they were doing the "*warsh*" and hanging them out to dry by the "*crick*." I still have a hard time saying yes to an invitation without saying, "*God willin' and the crick don't rise, I'll be there*." Is it a crick or a creek? I don't care. It will always be a crick to me.

When God gave me the word Unforsaken, I knew, it was the name of our ministry. To me, Unforsaken meant, I am never alone, and I am never going to be left alone, no matter what happens. Even if my worst-case scenario happens, I will not have to face it alone. I have Jesus. I am unforsaken. For some reason, that has done a heck of a lot of healing for this once, very, fearful and anxious girl.

Now that the ministry is 14 years old, Unforsaken means a ton of different things to a ton of different women and men. God has used that word that He created, that is still not called a real word, and He gave it legs to do whatever He sent it out to do.

The Bible says in Psalm 107:20, "*He sent out his word and healed them, and delivered them from their destruction.*" Oh, heck yes. That is the power of the spoken Word of God. Healing and deliverance from destruction? I want in! I need in. I don't want to go a day without being all in on that. That's the power of the Word and that's the power of acting in obedience to a word, that was spoken by Him to you, in the Secret Place.

Rest in The Secret Place

The Word says in Psalm 91:1, *"He who dwells in the shelter of the Most High will rest in the shadow of The Almighty."* (NIV) or if you refer to the King James Version we read, *"He that dwelleth in the secret place of the Most High shall abide under the shadow of the Almighty. (*KJV) In each version we read that there is a resting or abiding that needs to take place.

What does it mean to rest somewhere? Well, resting means abiding, which means, to stay somewhere, to sit still or to remain there. The word abide reminds me of the word abode, which means, a home. This scripture tells us to abide or rest in the shelter of The Most High, which is the shelter of God. We make God our home when we rest or abide with Him. God can become our safety and protection when we abide with Him under His wing.

Why in the world would we want our home anywhere else than right with God? God is all powerful, omniscient, omnipresent, unstoppable, and unbeatable. What other place would we want to call home than in the care of The Maker and Redeemer of all things.

Resting in the Secret Place promises us rest under His shadow. I don't know about you, but I need rest. My body is getting more and more tired each day. I am 51 years old. More gray hairs are coming in than blond, or let's be honest, brown, dyed to Champagne Blond as Loreal calls it.

I have new age spots on my arms and legs that are well deserved, as I enjoy the outdoors and the sunshine, and with that comes an abundance of healthy vitamin D, but also, skin that doesn't look the same as it did even 10 years ago.

I take about 7 vitamins each morning. This morning as I opened up each bottle, I said out loud, *"Ok, Lord, here they are, please let these do what they are supposed to."* Every day I take glucosamine and chondroitin for my joints, calcium and magnesium for my bones, a super supplemental multi, for my vitamins and minerals, iron for my blood, DHEA for my muscles, Pregnenolone for my moods (my husband is very thankful for this one), then I scooped a spoonful of collagen protein in my coffee for my hair, skin and nails. Those are just my morning vitamins.

I have a lovely cocktail of herbs my functional doctor put together for me to naturally calm my cortisol and estrogen down at night so I can sleep.

Have I always had to take this many vitamins? Nope! 20 and 30 years ago, my body just sort of popped back into shape quickly after I delivered my four kids, my hair just adjusted to whatever chemicals I chose to lighten or highlight it with, and my eyebrows grew back so thick after plucking, I secretly dreamed of a day they would stop. Well, I got my wish. I rarely have to pluck my eyebrows anymore. I have replaced that torturous time with lathering coconut oil all over my body to replenish the moisture that has just sort of disappeared into thin air like my ability to read a 20-font note without first putting on my reading glasses.

I can't run like I used to. As a young mother, I could carry a baby on my hip while cooking dinner and talking on the phone to a customer I sold makeup to while homeschooling my first grader at the kitchen table. Yes, my energy used to be endless, even after long nights of breastfeeding a colicky baby.

Now, I literally schedule my physical work on our farm and in ministry between the hours of 9am and 2pm, while my morning coffee and B12 vitamins are in full effect.

Between the hours of 2pm and 3pm, my afternoon consists of computer work, studying and writing or an occasional heavenly day in which I catch a couple episodes of The Waltons in between a nap. Yes, 2:00pm-3:00pm is my rejuvenation time.

I still have an evening of chores, dinner, dishes, and family obligations that will require me to be coherent and awake, so I have to be diligent about my afternoon rest. Otherwise, I appear like the lead character in the movie *"Weekend at Bernies."* (Oldie, but a goodie)

I thank God for His loving voice that spoke to me in My Secret Place one day telling me that it was *"Time to go to the doctors."* Yes, I knew it was time for bloodwork. After all, I hadn't had bloodwork done since I was pregnant with my now 19-year-old. How sad is that? We do that right? We, especially as women, make sure our husbands and our kids get their checkups, their dental cleanings, their chiropractic adjustments and medical attention, but when it comes to our health, we ignore that reminder in our journals over and over that reads, *"Make a doc apt."*

Why do we forget to rest? Why do we forget to take care of our bodies? You do know we were bought at a price, and our bodies are not our own, they belong to God, right? The Word says in 1

Corinthians 6:19, *"Do you not know that your body is a temple of the Holy Spirit, who is in you, whom you have received from God?"* We would never dream of littering or ignoring caring for our church building or temple, yet we litter our bodies with sugar and caffeine and fried foods and expect it to work the way it should.

I thank God I went to the doctor finally and had my bloodwork done. I have an amazing functional doctor who got me straightened out and on the right track in my body. Now, she's just working on getting my brain chemicals where they need to be through supplements. She has her work cut out for her there.

Yes, my doctor is the one who encouraged me to find a rest time in the middle of the day to give my body and my brain some rest. This rest allows my system to recharge. She studied my brain chemicals at all times of the day and night. It's done by a saliva test. She was able to measure hormone levels and see how my body chemicals react at certain times of the day. She showed me that my fight or flight hormone never seems to shut off. Even at 3am my brain is still in fight or flight mode. That made total sense to me as I have had to learn from The Lord over the past 30 years how to supernaturally rest in Him, cast my cares on Him and replace poor thinking with The Word of God.

Here's the really, cool thing. My doctor showed me that my numbers were all over the place during most of the day and the night in the natural and that my brain seems to be working harder than it should be most of the time. But then she said, *"Only at 7am in the morning are your brain chemical levels in their healthiest and optimum state."* Guess what I do at 7am every morning? I am in my Secret Place with The Most High. I am resting in God. I am in my quiet, devotion time with God. I said to her, *"That'll preach!"*

God supernaturally puts my thinking in order every morning. He levels out my brain chemicals and gives me a fresh start each sunrise when we are in The Word together and in prayer. The Most High God made my brain, and all the chemicals in it. And, In the shelter of His wing, He is healing and repairing my brain that has been damaged for so long by living in a fallen world.

This is called renewing your mind and it's biblical. Romans 12:1-2 says, *"Therefore I urge you, brothers, in view of God's mercy, to offer your bodies as living sacrifices, holy and pleasing to God this is your spiritual act of worship. Do not conform any longer to the patterns of this world but be transformed by the renewing of your mind."* My brain is learning how to not conform anymore to its old ways of working as I read, study, memorize, meditate on scripture, and pray without ceasing.

I will need to renew my mind every day of my life until I go to be with Jesus. That is if I want to live in peace and joy and abundance. That goes the same for you. The truth is we don't think right without the Word of God.

In our old natural self:

We worry.

We fret.

We fear.

We get anxious.

We try to control situations.

We obsess.

We play the victim.

We feel depressed.

We struggle with jealousy.

We lash out in anger.

We feed habits and addictions.

We feel insecure.

We overeat.

We undereat.

We question ourselves.

We question others.

Am I preaching to anyone yet? The truth is, we develop habits, hang ups and strongholds of the enemy when we aren't learning to rest in Him.

The Secret Place offers us rest. We can rest and rejuvenate our restless, tired soul when we abide in Jesus. John 14:27 says, *"Peace, I leave with you, my peace I give you. I do not give to you as the world gives. Do not let your hearts be troubled and do not be afraid."* Jesus wants to give us His peace. He knows we need it. He made us. He fashioned us. He walked among us and experienced everything that we have, and He feels our pain. He understands us and it's His desire to give us peace and rest.

Matthew 11:28-30, *"Come to me, all you who are weary and burdened and I will give you rest. Take my yoke upon you and learn from me, for I am gentle and humble in heart, and you will find rest for your souls. For my yoke is easy and my burden is light."*

Oh friend, are you weary or burdened about anything? Come on, let's be real. Do you sometimes feel overwhelmed by the demands and the trials of the day? I know I do. I know that I have to say over and over, quite often, "I trust You Jesus."

I must give God my burdens often. If not, it is too heavy of a yoke to carry on my own. I am weak without Him. This world is too heavy for any human to carry without A Secret Place to visit and unload sometimes.

The Secret Place is where my mind finds rest. I have sat on my swing and laughed with God, cried to God, held my breath with God while waiting for an answer to a petition.

In my Secret Place with Him I told Him I didn't understand why He didn't heal my 15-month-old great-niece of brain cancer. I couldn't see how that could possibly be His will that she dies so soon. I knew He already could read my heart and see I was disappointed, so why not bring it all out into the light with Him? That same Secret Place with Him has been where He has healed my soul that felt it would never be whole again after losing her.

The Secret Place has been where God has convicted me of sin, disciplined me for poor attitudes, an undisciplined tongue, or my most frequently practiced sin, impatience. He also has sat me down in sickness there when I haven't taken enough time to rest for my health.

The Secret Place has been my soft place to rest a blistered behind when God has had to spiritually pop me like a good Daddy should when His little girl is out of line.

The Secret place has been a place where God has captured my tears and soothed my emotions after finding myself burnt-out in ministry and wanting to avoid people all together. I couldn't even take a trip to the grocery store without first consulting my Jesus for enough strength to step out into my garage and put the keys in the ignition to go.

My Secret Place is now being used to rock my precious grandbabies that were prayed for years and years before this world would ever see their breathtaking faces in person. As I sit and rock them, I sing Jesus Loves Me, and Jesus Loves the Little Children to them as I speak prayers of faith and protection over them and promise them my eternal love.

Each day I speak my loved one's names out and place their names in each line of Psalm 91 claiming each promise specifically for them. In doing so, I can cast my cares and worries about them at the feet of Jesus and allow Him to know that I trust Him with them. After all, they each belong to Him anyways. I am simply a beneficiary of the blessings upon blessings of having them in my everyday life, while here on Earth.

My Secret Place with Jesus is where I sit morning after morning, afternoon after afternoon, evening after evening, or whenever my soul longs for time away with Jesus. It is my place to lay burdens down and allow Him to pick me up, embrace me with His Holy Kiss, get lost in His Word and drown myself in His mercy.

There's truly nowhere I would rather be than with my Jesus. Though my swing is my favorite place to sit, it's not the only place I meet with Him. Remember, we are to abide with Him. Abide means live. I can't live on my swing 24/7, but I can live with my Jesus 24/7, as He lives in me. Do not hold off communication with Him until you get into a specific location. He wants us to dwell with Him.

We are to pray without ceasing. He wants us to abide with Him. He wants us attached to Him. He's already closer than our next breath. He's never going to leave us and never going to forsake us. We are unforsaken. We simply can't forget that.

He that dwelleth in the Secret Place of the Most High will rest in the shadow of The Almighty. I am thankful for a God that wants us to rest in Him and with Him. I am thankful for the secrets He tells us in our Secret Place.

Serving God

Serving God shouldn't be as complicated as we make it. Seminars and conventions and books upon books of leadership skills can bombard and distract us as disciples if we aren't careful.

Jesus was the perfect example of a Servant. The Bible actually refers to Him as The Suffering Servant.

Why do we look all over the place for examples of what to do and how to do it, when The Word of God lays it all out simply? Jesus sat with The Father then He served. Then He sat with The Father then He served.

You say, *"Well, Mo, He was Jesus, He could do anything He wanted to, He didn't have all these church members driving Him nuts with their agendas."* I would say to that, *"Um, yes He did."* Mark 1:32-38 shows this plainly.

"That evening after sunset the people brought to Jesus all the sick and demon possessed. The whole town gathered at the door, and Jesus healed many who had various diseases. He also drove out many demons, but he would not let the demons speak because they knew who he was.

Very early in the morning, while it was still dark, Jesus got up, left the house and went off to a solitary place, where he prayed. Simon and his companions went to look for him, and when they found him, they exclaimed: "Everyone is looking for you!"

Jesus replied, "Let us go somewhere else—to the nearby villages—so I can preach there also. That is why I have come."

Jesus had to teach His disciples how to minister correctly by ministering correctly. He got up before dark and escaped the people and got quiet in prayer. That is just the thing we are called to do. Look at what it says in vs 37. *"And when they found Him, they exclaimed, "Everyone is looking for You."* Jesus was purposely leaving the people to spend time in prayer, but the people didn't want to respect His boundaries. The people wanted His service.

This happens so often to true servants of Jesus if they remain addicted to people's opinions of them. People-pleasing can suck the pure love you have for people right out of you if you don't purposely escape the people and get alone with The Father often.

People will never get enough of your service if you do not draw healthy boundaries yourself. Take it from a recovering people-pleasing addict, you can't do this marathon called *"The ministry of reconciliation"* well if you are constantly allowing the people to steal your rest in The Lord.

You need to get alone and quiet with God often if you want to properly serve Him. You can't serve from an empty cup. You need Him to fill you up so you can pour out again.

When these disciples told Him the people were looking for Him, Jesus said *"Let us go somewhere else-to the nearby villages-so I can preach there also. That is why I have come."* Jesus didn't come to earth to cast out demons and heal the sick. He did that, yes, but it's not why He came. He came to draw the sinners to repentance and turn the hearts of the people to The Father. He came to rescue humanity from death and save our souls from Hell. That kind of calling required resting in The Father's care often.

If Jesus needed rest and time with The Father, who do we think we are, not taking time to sit? It's a pride thing when we don't get alone with God and just keep serving in our own power. We can't do it very long without Him.

I know I never want to ever do that again.
Rest in Him, then let Him make you a vessel fit for service.

Attached To Jesus

John 15:5 *"I am The Vine; you are the branches. If a man remains in me and I in him, he will bear much fruit; apart from Me, you can do nothing."*

My daughter Sara is our only daughter. Tommy and I had three boys and a girl. We had two boys first, then our Sara, then one more boy. When our youngest was born, Sara hoped for a sister. She was not happy to find out he was a boy. It didn't take her long to change her tune though when she realized that as the only girl, she could step into her rightful role as second mother in the home. She bossed those boys around something fierce. I would have to remind her, *"Sara, I am the mom."*

I am grateful beyond words that I have a special relationship with each of my children. My boys are each unique and special and the apple of my eye in every way, shape, and form. Sara, she is my girl. She has been my shadow since birth. Sara has been attached to my hip for as long as I can remember. Sara never wanted to be put down. She hated the stroller, the walker, the bouncy seat. She only wanted me. She required a lot of attention and affection. I mainly remember nursing Sara or holding her. She was literally, always attached to me.

As a toddler, Sara was probably my hardest child. It's ok that I say this. She has heard it a million times. She did not like the word *"no."* If I said *"no"* to my boys their little lips would quiver, and they would stop whatever they were doing and obey.

They were so submissive and obedient. Sara, on the other hand, had a better idea of how to do whatever she was doing at the time. She had a strong will, and she still does today. She spent more time in time-out than all three of my boys combined.

I clearly remember when I finally realized that Sara was a stronger leader than me. It was her 15th birthday party. Until this time, she had always allowed me to give her a party and make a lot of decisions for the party. She would tell me what she wanted, and I would just run with the theme or idea. On this 15th birthday, I remember arguing with her over and over about every detail of the party. It was miserable.

My husband Tommy finally took me aside and said, *"Hon, why don't you just let her plan it?"* I said, *"What? Plan her own party? Isn't that weird?"* I had never experienced this before. It was that day, The Holy Spirit showed me that Sara is stronger than me and a much better leader. I literally handed her the reigns and she has been the Family Party Planner ever since.

Sara is now the Operations Director for our ministry. She does most of the planning for the ministry as well. She is my boss now and I love it. It's better. She's a natural leader and she's been trying to lead since she could kick. I simply couldn't let her do it at three years old.

The ministry is thriving now, and God knew what He was doing giving me that strong willed child. I tell young moms all the time that if they have a child that just seems to live in time-out, take heart, they are future leaders.

Sara and I work together in the ministry, but more than that, she is my everyday buddy. She calls me about ten times a day. Though there is no special ring on my phone for her, my husband and I can almost tell it's her when the phone rings.

She loves to Face-time so we can see each other too. Now that she has two kids, I adore this even more as I get little glimpses of my grandbabies all day long.

I thank God for that clingy little baby and bossy little toddler that she was, as her attachment to me was not simply because of her desire to lead, it was also her desire to learn. She's been watching me and emulating me her whole life. When she speaks somewhere on stage or on video, she is constantly told, *"You sound just like your mom."* I'm sure that annoys her sometimes. It doesn't me. It's such a compliment to me.

She's truthfully my *"why"* many days. When I want to be short tempered, or give up in an area, I remind myself Sara is watching. I pursue purity and holiness because I want Sara to. I work hard because I want Sara to. I love God and people because I want Sara to. Of course, I want that for all my kids and grandchildren.

I try to set a great example for all of them. But my boys have an amazing Godly Dad to emulate. I feel that Sara's mentoring is my responsibility as a woman of God and as her mother.

Sara learned a lot from me by staying attached to me. She was as close to me as a daughter could be until it was time for her to go to school and begin making decisions on her own. She stayed in the shadow of my wing while I stayed in the shadow of God's wing. Sara abided with me. It's in abiding that we learn and grow and thrive. It's in abiding with Jesus that we are safe, secure and able to produce fruit.

John 15:5 says, *"I am the Vine, and you are the branches. If a man remains in me and I in him, he will bear much fruit; apart from me you can do nothing."* Abiding or remaining in God is vital for our production of fruit. What does God mean by fruit? Well, it doesn't take an expert gardener to recognize the difference in a fruit-filled tree or bush and one that has nothing but leaves and branches.

The truth is, people can live in this world and never even mention the Name Jesus, never step foot into a church, never close their eyes and pray.

 Countless people in this world walk through every day of their lives thinking this world is it. They do not believe in God. They do not believe that The Bible is the Word of God. They do not believe in Heaven or Hell. They simply are living day to day focused on this life, all it has to offer in about 70-80 years and then they believe they will just die and be done.

What a tragedy if no one reaches them with the truth. What a tragedy if they miss out on our true meaning of existence which is to glorify God with our lives. What a tragedy if they never speak the

Name of Jesus until Judgement Day when they will face a very bitter truth that Jesus is Lord and that they did not choose Him while they were alive.

What a tragedy when they realize that this world is not it. Our last breath here on Earth is only the beginning of our eternal destinies. Heaven for those who call Jesus Lord, Hell for those who don't.

There is no fruit bearing in a life lived absent of The Vinedresser. Only by being attached to The Father, through a relationship with Jesus can anyone produce fruit that will last. Vines can grow all day long, even if they don't produce any fruit. Take it from a country girl. There are countless vines growing all over our pasture that do nothing but stretch out and attempt to absorb nutrients from other plants that are fruit producing. They are green, but useless. This kind of sounds like the world a little to me.

Take heed that you aren't trying to live a fruitful life among a bunch of weeds and fruitless vines. Jesus tells us to abide in Him and to have His Words abide in us, this is when we will produce fruit. No Jesus, No fruit. Know Jesus, Know fruit.

What does He mean by abiding? Recently I taught about this in a teaching I was doing about

Overcoming Fear in The Secret Place with God.
What does abiding mean? Well, abiding means:

Staying

Resting

Not leaving

Dwelling

Living (Think about the word abode, which means a dwelling place or a home)

If we abide in the shelter of The Most High, we will rest in the shadow of The Almighty. When we truly stay always attached to God in prayer, talking to Him, petitioning Him, praising Him, including Him in our everyday lives, we can rest. We can rest from worry, rest from fear, rest from striving in our own meaningless efforts.

Abiding means never leaving. When we can learn to do what Paul talks about when He says, *"Pray without ceasing"* in 1 Thessalonians 5:16, we can truthfully experience a fruitful life. Fruit meaning, the fruits of the Spirit come alive in us like never before: love, peace, patience, kindness, faithfulness, goodness and self-control. When these fruits are present, we experience the abundant life God wants for us.

Fear is killed in the Secret Place with God. Anxiety is demolished in The Secret Place with God. Depression must flee in the Secret Place with God. This happens when we take what we learn in prayer and study, and we put it into practice with Jesus.

The Word says in Matthew 6:6, *"But you, when you pray, go into your room, and when you have shut your door, pray to your Father who sees in the Secret Place; and your Father Who sees in secret will reward you openly."* Matthew 6:6. (NKJV)

Oh, my goodness, I am excited to dissect this with you. What does this mean to me? It means, God is truly the only One Who truthfully knows ALL our fears. I don't care what counselor you go to, what 12 steps you are working through, what best friend or confident with skin you are able to open up to, only God knows ALL of your fears. We do not ever completely share with another human *everything* that we are dealing with. We can't, out of fear of rejection or abandonment. God knows though.

God knows what we can't even say out loud. He knows the very beatings of our hearts. He knows our innermost thoughts before we think them. Psalm 139:1-2 reads, *"O LORD, you have searched me and known me! You know when I sit down and when I rise up; you discern my thoughts from afar."* God knows it all. He knows what we haven't repented for yet. He knows what we haven't revealed to Him yet. He knows what we haven't forgiven someone for yet. He knows. He knows, yet He waits for us to get 100% truthful with Him. He doesn't rush us. He waits for us in The Secret Place. God heals us from our fears in The Secret Place. We can get totally healed when we finally get totally real. You have to get real to heal. I always say, *"If it rhymes, it's from God."*

Do I advocate counseling? Oh, goodness, yes. I think everyone in the world could benefit from a good Christian counselor. Do I advocate a 12 step Christian program for hurts or habits? Oh goodness yes. Some of the most amazing saints in the Kingdom right now have found their faith and strength at an effective program. Do I advocate being involved in a small group? Oh, goodness, yes.

We are built for community. We need others to hold our arms up in prayer and intercession while we grow and heal. Do I advocate being active in a local church? Oh, goodness, yes. The Church is God's Bride. Jesus is serious about His Bride, and whatever Jesus is serious about, we should be. The local church is the hope of a lost and dying world. We need to be involved at a local church.

I am an advocate for all these things, but nothing that you learn in any of these other avenues will make any lasting change in your life, unless you work it out in your Secret Place with God in prayer and action.

In the Secret Place, head knowledge becomes heart knowledge. In the Secret Place, God takes our knowledge, He mixes it with His anointing and His Word, and it becomes true wisdom. In the Secret Place while praying to the Father, we can put into practice privately every bit of training we get corporately.

1 John 2:20-27 reads, *"But you have an anointing from the Holy One, and all of you know the truth. I do not write to you because you do not know the truth, but because you do know it and because no lie comes from the truth. Who is the liar? It is whoever denies that Jesus is the Christ. Such a person is the antichrist—denying the Father and the Son. No one who denies the Son has the*

Father; whoever acknowledges the Son has the Father also.

As for you, see that what you have heard from the beginning remains in you. If it does, you also will remain in the Son and in the Father. And this is what he promised us—eternal life". I am writing these things to you about those who are trying to lead you astray. As for you, the anointing you received from him remains in you, and you do not need anyone to teach you. But as his anointing teaches you about all things and as that anointing is real, not counterfeit—just as it has taught you, remain in him".

Remain in Him.

Stay in Him.

Abide in Him.

Dwell in The Secret place of The Most High, with Him.

Stay attached to Him.

A New Thing

If I have learned anything over the past 31 years of being a mother and now a Mimi, it is to say that nothing ever stays the same and change is inevitable. Lately God had kind of given me a crash course in not focusing on the past and pressing on to what is coming next, in our family life and in ministry. Change causes us to either fret or trust! I have decided to trust, and God is so good, He has given me such supernatural joy in the trusting. Isaiah 43:18-19 reads, *"Forget the former things, do not dwell on the past. See, I am doing a new thing. Now it springs up do you not perceive it? I am making a way in the desert and streams in the wasteland."*

Forget the former things, do not dwell on the past. That's a lot easier said than done, right? There's something about our past that can trip us up quicker than we can say photo album. Yes, we can get hung up on yesterday when yesterday was good, and we can get hung up on yesterday when yesterday caused us trauma of some sort.

We as humans tend to remember the really, good and the really, bad. There's something strange that happens to the average, everyday ordinary things. They sort of fade away in our memories.

But friend, can I tell u something? The older I get, the more I am working on cherishing the everyday, average, ordinary days. I'm beginning to recognize the blessing of enjoying everyday life. Not just special days and holidays. Not just weekends and days off. Not just traveling or on vacation. It is God's will that we enjoy every day whether sunshine or rain.

John 10:10 says, "*The thief comes to steal, kill and destroy. I've come so that you may have life and have it more abundantly.*" God wants us to live everyday with an abundance of Joy. Living joy-filled lives is God's will for all of us.
Forget the former things do not dwell on the past. God is serious about us freeing ourselves from the shackles of our past. We even must let go of the good things sometimes to let God fill us with better things.

I have a garden. One of the hardest things I've had to learn in gardening is that pruning is ok. Pruning is one of the best things you can do for a healthy plant to make it even more fruitful. I was so scared to trim my pretty bushes and flowers at first because it seemed like if something is doing well you should just leave it alone. But the truth is, when we prune a plant back and make bouquets with the clippings, the plants get stronger each time.

It's basically the same way with us. The Word says, *"I am the true vine, and my Father is the gardener. He cuts off every branch in me that bears no fruit, while every branch that does bear fruit, he prunes so that it will be even more fruitful."* (John 15:1-2 NIV) God's will for us to be fruitful and multiply even though we are producing fruit somewhere, sometimes means God will prune us so we can be more fruitful.

You know, sometimes God must strip back some good things from us, so that we can walk in the great things that He has for us.

As I think about our service in church, serving in the nursery is good fruit, greeting at the front door at church is good fruit, and working on the outreach team is good fruit. But, if you are doing all these good things, and God has called you to sing on the worship team, or help with youth, God may call you to prune some of these other good things that are keeping you from the best thing, which is walking in obedience to His desires for you.

I have pretty much in one season or another helped in every area of ministry. Well, except singing. God knows I wanted that gift, but it just wasn't Gods will. I think He knew if I could carry a tune, I would try to hit it big in country on the

Nashville strip. I am pretty sure my inability to harmonize is for my own good.

Yes, I have served all over, and many times I've gotten so far in over my head serving in so many areas, if God tried to speak to me what He wanted me to be doing, I probably wouldn't hear Him clearly over my busyness. Friend, there is a lovely word that some of us need to learn and start using. It starts with an N and ends with an O.

No! Let's say that together. We can say it nicely. We can say:
No, thank you.
No, I'm sorry
No, I just don't feel God leading me to do that.
No, it's just a different season for me.

Good job! You know, no isn't a bad word. Saying no to tons of good things helps us to say yes to the best things with God. I always coach other serve-a-holics like myself by teaching them that if you sign up to do everything, you are taking a serving spot from someone God is actually calling to do it.

An obedient heart and a serving heart are beautiful. But friends, let's not forget to take time to ask God where, when, and in what capacity He wants us serving in. He's the boss, applesauce!

"For I desire mercy, not sacrifice, and acknowledgment of God rather than burnt offerings." (Hosea 6:6 NIV) God may call you to let go of some things you have done or loved doing in the past because He has something bigger and better for you in the future. I want to encourage you to not let the fear of change block your blessing.

Let God prune.
Let God do His work.
He knows what He's doing.

In the ministry whenever God has built something, and I've been blessed to be a part of it, it's never been easy to pass the torch when God has called me to trust someone else with it. I've had to learn to step out and say, *Yes Lord*! Honestly, I usually pass it feeling fear but pressing through it. Then later I look back and say Praise God! He knew what He was doing.

When I think of Unforsaken Women's resale shop. I remember When God told me to give my daughter Sara the management position of the store and then told me to step down and get back home to write and teach. I remember that It was scary for me, but I look back now at how great she did and how wonderful our present manager is doing.

The store looks better. It's thriving in sales. It is the primary support for the entire ministry. The volunteers love serving there. The food pantry at the store is feeding hungry people on a daily basis. The community is excited about the shop. It truly was God saying, "Pass it on." Trust God's pruning. He's working on fruitfulness.

Maybe you need me to tell you today, *"Let it go."* It's God's anyways. No matter what it is. Every good and perfect gift comes from Him. He owns it all. Everything belongs to Jesus anyways. We must remember this. It's pride sometimes that keeps us stuck in the past, not able to let go and move on.

Pride says I made this. Trust says God made this.
Pride says It will fail without me. Trust says If God built it, God will take care of it
Pride says me. Trust says He.
I always say, *"If it rhymes, it's from God."*

I don't care how good it is. How good it was or how strange and scary it feels to let it go. If God says, *"Forget the former things do not dwell on the past."* Forget it. Let it go. Hand it to God. Don't dwell on it.

Where we dwell, we stay. If you keep dwelling on past blessings you get stuck there and can miss the new blessings God has for you.

I've only been talking about getting stuck in the past good things and not letting God take us to our new things. Truthfully, often, it's the mistakes and the regrets and the failures of the past that we hold onto so tightly. God sometimes must pry our hands open spiritually trying to get us to loosen these memories and traumas so He can place His love, and forgiveness, and peace, and joy, and next things in them.

When we can't let go of the past, we steal our present peace, and we paralyze our future prosperity.

The Word says, *Whom the son sets free is free indeed.*
The Word says, *Forgive and you will be forgiven.*
The Word says, *I will forgive all your sins and heal all your diseases*
The Word says, *He who overcomes Will be dressed in white. I will never blot out their names from the book of life.*
The Word says, *The Son of Man has the power to forgive sins*
The Word says *that your sins will be as far from you as the east is from the west and they are buried in the sea of forgetfulness to be remembered no more.*

If God has forgiven us and forgotten our sins, can we please stop reminding him of them? Can we stop telling God how messed up we are? Can we stop telling God we are so sorry for those things He's already forgotten? Can we stop reminding Him how unworthy we are?
Because my bible tells me that
We are forgiven.
We are redeemed.
We are restored.
We are new.
We are clean.

"Then he showed me Joshua the high priest standing before the angel of the Lord, and Satan standing at his right side to accuse him. The Lord said to Satan, "The Lord rebuke you, Satan! The Lord, who has chosen Jerusalem, rebuke you! Is not this man a burning stick snatched from the fire?" Now Joshua was dressed in filthy clothes as he stood before the angel. The angel said to those who were standing before him, "Take off his filthy clothes." Then he said to Joshua, "See, I have taken away your sin, and I will put fine garments on you." Then I said, "Put a clean turban on his head." So, they put a clean turban on his head and clothed him, while the angel of the Lord stood by."
Zechariah 3:1-5 NIV

My friend, stop putting those old shoes on your new feet. Take off those filthy garments. The Lord has already snatched you from the fire. Get your eyes off the past. If your past mistakes from ten minutes ago are stealing your joy, Let it go! If your past mistakes from 10 years ago are stealing your joy, let it go!

We must keep our eyes straight ahead. When we look back, we trip, Face forward! Stop letting the past trip you. I promise, I am preaching to myself as well.

The Apostle Paul got it. He knew he couldn't look back at where God had rescued him. He had to face forward. Paul was a murderer and a persecutor of Christians when God called him. Paul knew and said about himself in so many words, *I am the worst of sinners and if God can save me, If God can forgive me, If God can redeem me, If God can use me, He can use anybody.*

Paul says in Philippians 3:13-14
"Brothers and sisters, I do not consider myself yet to have taken hold of it. But one thing I do: Forgetting what is behind and straining toward what is ahead, I press on toward the goal to win the prize for which God has called me heavenward in Christ Jesus."

We, like Paul, must press on. To press on requires effort. We aren't always going to feel forgiven, but we press on knowing we are forgiven. We aren't always going to feel like a new creation. But we press on and walk out our lives as new creations.

We aren't always going to feel like God loves us. But we press on and accept that unconditional love because If God's Word says it's true, it's true. I think God knew the Apostle Paul would struggle with his past, so God had to change his name. His name wasn't always, Paul. He was Saul. God renamed him when He called him. God has done that a few times in The Bible.

If changing your name will help you finally let go of that old baggage and begin to walk in your peace and forgiveness and strength Christ died for you to walk in, then, change your name.

Whatever you must do, choose to forget the former things and not dwell on the past. Right now, say out loud to yourself, *let it go*! Forget the former things do not dwell on the past.

Isaiah 43:19 reads, *"See, I'm doing a new thing. Do you not perceive it? "It's time for our new thing."* Habakkuk 1:5 reads, *"Look at the nations and watch and be utterly amazed. For I am going to do something in your days that you would not believe, even if you were told."* I love the Word. I feel like God is saying, *"Listen, you aren't even going to believe what I'm going to do, it's going to be so amazing."*

This can't even come close to explaining something supernatural that God is doing, but when I think of this scripture, I think of the first time you take someone to Disney World and maybe they are an adult and have never been. They have been to fairs and other theme parks but never Disney. I think it's just as much fun for the person watching someone see it for the first time. But as you're driving there with them, you're like *"you're not going to believe how awesome it is."*

The Word says, *"I'm doing something new; can you perceive it?"* The definition of Perceive is: Become aware of, conscious of or to realize or understand.

Here goes God getting us pumped up. Like, *can you even imagine?*
You don't realize what I'm going to do. You don't understand!
I'm doing something new that you won't even be able to handle, it's so great.
Let go of the past because anything new I do have to be in a new container.

Mark 2:21-22 says. *"No one sews a patch of unshrunk cloth on an old garment. Otherwise, the new piece will pull away from the old, making the tears worse. And no one pours new wine into old wineskins. Otherwise, the wine will burst the skin, and both the wine and the wineskins will be ruined. No, they pour new wine into new wineskins."* My friend, can you perceive God doing something new? Can you get excited about it? Can you handle it?

Some people can picture new things. Some people can't. I am kind of the queen of trash to treasure. I love old things made new. I would 100x more love an old piece of furniture, or an old house restored or an old piece of anything made into new than just going out and buying something new.

 I can spot a treasure on the side of the road that the world has just tossed to the curb. I can envision a little sanding and painting. You know, a little caulk and a little paint makes things what they ain't! I can envision a treasure in waiting. So can God!

Our God can see a drug attic and envision a pastor.
Our God can see a prostitute and envision an evangelist.

105

Our God can see a borderline Agoraphobic, anxious mess, and He can picture an author and ministry leader who will help women renew their minds in the Word.

You see, God doesn't focus on our pasts. He sees our future when He begins His work with us. He sees us covered in Jesus' blood and washed clean. He sees us wearing our Robes of Righteousness because we belong to Jesus. Yes, Our God Starts from the end with us and works forward. He makes us Holy before we act holy. He makes us righteous while we are still acting like we are sinners. He secures our Heavenly dwelling while we are still trying to live out our lives here. God starts with our end in mind.

You know, we must run our race that way. We must fix our eyes on the prize the entire time. We must fix our eyes on Jesus the author and finisher of our faith.

Isaiah 43:18-19 says, *"Forget the former things. Do not dwell on the past. See, I'm doing a new thing. Now it springs up; do you not perceive it? I am making a way in the desert and streams in the wasteland."*

God is the one that is doing it. You don't have to worry about figuring out how to do it, God does. You don't even have to understand how He will do this new thing? You just must perceive it. You don't have to make streams in the wasteland, God does.

God does the miracles. You must have faith. You must let go and let God.

I love that song. *Waymaker.* The words say, *"Waymaker, Miracle Worker, Promise Keeper, Light in the Darkness, My God, That is Who you are."* You and I don't have to know how to make the way. God makes it. We don't have to understand miracles. We can't, it's supernatural! We don't have to provide light in the darkness, that's God's job. We just shine His light. We don't have to understand how God does it. He makes the way in the desert. He makes streams in the wasteland. He's the Waymaker.

He just simply asks us to forget the past and let Him do this new thing. He just wants us to allow Him to make new ways, trudge new paths, create His treasure from our trash we have made of things.

He does the transforming. We just do the trusting. He is able. The Bible tells us He is more than able. According to Ephesians 3:*20 "He is able to do exceedingly and abundantly more than we can ask or imagine according to His power that is at work In us."* It's His ability, and His power. But He's placed that power in us. He's placed that way making, miracle working, light in the darkness, power on the inside of us, because we carry Holy Spirit.

We have His power at work on the inside of us and we simply must allow God to show us what He wants to do in and through us. You and I are containers of supernatural power. Can you perceive it?

We must let God prune when He wants to prune. He knows what He's doing. He's creating fruit. We must stop bucking against the changes that God is wanting to do in and through our lives. These changes are required for the new blessings to come. Trust Him.

We must let go of that old baggage that we have been dragging around for decades so God can hand us our new adventures. We must let it go, trust Him and let it go right now.

He's doing it. Trust Him. It's going to be so good. I promise. I know the end of the story we win. We get to be with Him. We get to walk on streets of gold. We get to be reunited with our loved ones.

We get the ultimate victory. So, until then, let's press on toward the prize.

We are surrounded by a great cloud of witnesses who are cheering us on. Let's fix our eyes on Jesus, The Author and Perfector of our faith and let's run our race. He's making a way for us there. Can you perceive it?

That's Not How He Sees Me

I remember having the same conversation with almost all four of my kids and a few of my nieces and nephews. The scene usually takes place with me reaching out because I know something is bothering them. I hear them say, *"It just must be me."* And of course, this protective Mama or Auntie in some cases says, *"No honey, it's not you. It's just not who God has planned for you right now."*

Most of them graduated from High School, where they were a big fish in a small pond, only to find themselves in college, living at home, or on their own and working to pay themselves through school, encountering the hum drum of real life, and wondering if they are on the right path.

They envision all their friends having completely figured this life thing out already, I mean, after all, they seem happy on Instagram. Which, is a one hundred percent accurate measure of people's lives after all, right? I think you can sense my sarcasm, as someone who fights my detest of social media and its implications on our self-esteem quite often.

It's usually about a relationship. Someone they were interested in, just stopped texting them, or as they call it, *"ghosted"* them. They wonder why they aren't even worthy of the closure of a fake excuse of, *"It's not you, it's me."* Then, this Mama or Auntie must fight her inner desire to run and fight their battles, secretly reaching out to the "ghoster" telling them how incredibly stupid they are not to want to continue a relationship with my son or my daughter or loved one.

Instead, I minister to them the same way I minister to every woman I encounter who is hurting. I share a true struggle that I have been through and how I watched God show up in His amazing way to rescue me from my mess. Because the truth is, I have been in some ugly messes, usually brought on by my own insecurity, desire to feel worthy or my fear of being alone.

I share that I kissed a lot of frogs before God brought me my Prince. I tell of how badly I wanted to be loved that I settled for less than God's best for me. I share this, and plead with them not to settle, but to do what took me years and years of pain and disappointment to figure out how to do. I plead with them to pursue Jesus and let God bring them their partner.

If it's something besides a relationship issue, I still minister the same way. I tell them how I did it wrong until I learned how to do it right or am still learning to do it right with God.

I encourage them to heal like I do by studying His Word and seeing what His instruction book tells us to do in any and every situation, especially concerning living in fellowship with other humans here on this big old planet.

We usually end the conversation with praying together. I can remember being down on the floor with a couple of my sweet, loved ones begging God to show her or him just how much they are loved by Him. I beg Him to show them just how beautifully and wonderfully they are made in His image. I storm the throne room of Heaven alongside them saying, *"Daddy, show her how beautiful she is to you." "Show him, he is Your son." "Show her that's not how you see her."*

Because that's what He's had to do for me. He has had to show me, I am His. I'm His girl. I'm not the hot mess I feel like. That's not how He sees me. And it's not how He sees you.

I thank God that I was able to have these courageous conversations with my loves. I thank God that when I sensed they were hurting, I didn't just ignore it and go about my business, but I reached out to say, *"Hey, can we talk?"* I thank

God that each one of these precious souls know just how loved they are by me, but even more important than that, they know, they are priceless to God.

He's enamored with them. He is crazy about them. And He proved it by paying the ultimate price for them. He gave His all. He gave His Son. *"But God demonstrates his own love for us in this: While we were still sinners, Christ died for us"* *(Romans 5:8)*

Most of them are married to Godly spouses now, and the others will be soon enough. The best news is, they now know, it isn't them. They aren't busted, broken and beyond being loved. It's completely the opposite.

They are loved, cherished, and set apart for God. They have learned the lesson it took me years and years to learn. That's not how He sees me.

Just Love

I love summer! I'm one of those weird people that loves the heat. I love humidity. I hate cold, dry weather. My hair and skin feel so soft in the summer from the humidity and in the winter, I feel like an old, dried up, leather bag. I know I shouldn't complain as I live in Florida. But, even living in Florida, the winters feel too cold to me.

I know most Floridians look forward to the cooler months, so they don't have to turn on the AC. Not me, I love the summer when the sun shines till late in the day. I love watching it rise each day and watching it set late in the evening.

I love the smell of sunscreen, mixed with the smell of the BBQ grill going and I even like the sweat running down my back as I garden. It's like I'm multi-tasking, growing healthy food to eat, while at the same time, getting toxins out of my body.

I even love the summer rainstorms here in Florida. I love sitting on my porch swing (my secret place) and soaking in the sound of the rain on our metal roof. It's truly my peace. I'll sit there and watch my cows and goats in the pasture and just listen for God's voice. He speaks to us in such beautiful ways, doesn't He? Lately God has been using

nature and animals and gardening to reach and teach me. He is so good.
He's our Creator, Sustainer, Healer, Deliverer.

He is so full of love. He can't help Himself from loving us. It's Who He is. It's His essence. Do you know you are loved beyond your wildest comprehension?

It's the truth. The Maker of Heaven and Earth, who made the stars and the moon and the sun and the mountains and seas and landscape, that Maker is in love with you. He created you, designed you, fashioned you, and anointed you. He's enamored with you. He loves you and He loves me, and there's nothing we can do about it.

You are loved perfectly. We are called to love God and love people. Loving God is easy. But we can't love others correctly until we learn how to accept the love God has for us. It's easy to love Him all day, He's loveable. But we also need to learn how to properly accept His love for us so we can love others correctly. We love because He first loved us.

My cow knows how to give and accept love. They all do. I have a pasture full of heifers. Do you know that that means? Heifers are pretty much, hormonal girls. Girls that act lovely 90% of the month, but when it's time for them to go into heat, they stand at the fence with their butts facing the road looking for love in all the wrong places. They moo and irritate the other girls in the herd. They are kind of like college girls who wear too little clothes to the club at night trying to get a guy to pay attention to them. You know what I mean. I can say that, because I was one of those girls one time in the past. Way in the past, before I knew Jesus.

Truthfully, every creature on Earth, especially humans, is searching for love and we search in the wrong places when we rely on our instincts and senses to lead us.

We as new creatures in Christ must learn to give and accept the love God has for us in healthy, mature ways. We can't just rely on our 5 senses and instincts like animals. God has given us His Spirit to guide us. We must be Spirit led.

We learn about God's love by reading our Word and spending time with Him in fellowship and by slowing our roles and sitting still long enough to allow Him to pour His love on us. Not by standing at fences in life demanding our needs be met instantly. We will always be searching for Love until we find Jesus. God created our hearts like a vacuum. Nothing will fill that empty space or that God shaped hole correctly except Jesus.

Until we learn how to receive His love properly, we will try a zillion other cheap substitutes to feel some temporary peace. These fillers are called idols. We will try to worship things like:
Shopping
Or money
Or gambling
Or exercise
Or food
Or getting our hair done or nails done
Or people
We will try to fill that hole with anything or everything until we finally realize that none of these things will fill us forever except God's love. Only in a personal relationship with Jesus will we truly be made whole. The Word says, *"God so loved the world that He gave His Son". (John 3:16)* Our relationship with Jesus has always been God's intentional fulfillment to all our yearnings in life.

God desires that we receive that love and learn how to walk in that love and allow that love to heal us from the inside out, then intentionally share that love with others. 1 John 3:1-2 says *"See what great love the Father has lavished on us, that we*

*should be called children of God! And that is what
we are! The reason the world does not know us is
that it did not know him."* My friend, God has
lavished His love on us by making us children of
God, Co-heirs with Christ, Sons and Daughters of
The Kingdom. God gave us this love and He
expects that we learn how to accept this love and
share it with others.

Nothing makes me feel more loved by God than in
those quiet, still times with Him in prayer.
In our quiet times:
He stills our souls,
quiets our minds,
heals our bodies and hearts,
renews us and makes us stronger,
God's love for us is lavished on us as His children.
I don't know about you, but I can't help but love
my kids. I am enamored with my kids and when I
say my kids you know by now after reading this
book, that includes my grands. They are a part of
my kids, the best parts of them.

Remember, I told you that I have three two-year-
old grandbabies right now and that three of my
kids all had babies in the same year. Sometimes
when I'm talking about the two-year-olds, even
though they are cousins, I call them the triplets. I
texted all of my kids recently and said, *"Well, the*

triplets are all two. Just so you know these have been the best 5 years of my life, being a Mimi".

I want to lavish love on my husband and kids and grands. And I'm a flawed hot mess human. Can you imagine how God wants to love us? He's the epitome of love. He wants nothing less than for us to receive His Perfect love.

 1 John 4:16 reads, *"And so we know and rely on the love God has for us. God is love. Whoever lives in love lives in God, and God in them.* He is love, and this right here says, *if we live in love we are living in Him."*

Truthfully, we can't do a dang good thing of lasting value without Him. If we do good, it's God doing it through us. We better not get ourselves all puffed up and in pride when we do good. Apart from Him, the Word says we can do nothing. 1 John 4:19 says, *"We love because He first loved us".*

I could venture to guess that 99% of people struggling with addictions or incarcerated or struggling in strongholds are where they are in their pain because they never truthfully, and deep down, ever learned how loved they were by their Creator. Not just loved, perfectly loved. That is why we need to run to as many as we can to share with them the love God has for them so they can heal completely.

No story in the Bible represents this better than the story of The Prodigal Son.
In Luke 15 we read.
"Jesus continued: "There was a man who had two sons. The younger one said to his father, 'Father, give me my share of the estate.' So, he divided his property between them. "Not long after that, the younger son got together all he had, set off for a distant country and there squandered his wealth in wild living. After he had spent everything, there was a severe famine in that whole country, and he began to be in need. So, he went and hired himself out to a citizen of that country, who sent him to his fields to feed pigs. He longed to fill his stomach with the pods that the pigs were eating, but no one gave him anything. "When he came to his senses, he said, 'How many of my father's hired servants have food to spare, and here I am starving to death! I will set out and go back to my father and say to him: Father, I have sinned against heaven and against you. I am no longer worthy of being called your son; make me like one of your hired servants.' So, he got up and went to his father. "But while he was still a long way off, his father saw him and was filled with compassion for him; he ran to his son, threw his arms around him and

kissed him. "The son said to him, 'Father, I have sinned against heaven and against you. I am no longer worthy to be called your son.' "But the father said to his servants, 'Quick! Bring the best robe and put it on him. Put a ring on his finger and sandals on his feet. Bring the fattened calf and kill it. Let's have a feast and celebrate. For this son of mine was dead and is alive again, he was lost and is found.' So, they began to celebrate."
Luke 15:11-24 NIV

The Father in The Parable of the Prodigal Son didn't wait for His Son to come graveling home to him, he saw his son way off in the distance heading back and he hiked up his robe and he ran to him.

The Father of The Prodigal Son is God. His love is shown to His Son through outrageous generosity and irrational kindness. He didn't treat his son as he deserved to be treated. He treated him as His love for him commanded Him to treat him. His mercy and His grace trumped his judgement. God doesn't treat us as our sins deserve us to be treated. He loves us unconditionally.

We are called to love like that. God intends for us to learn to receive this love correctly, not to just feel good and heal ourselves, but to receive His Perfect love and share it with others. 1 John 4:11

says, *"Dear friends, since God so loved us, we also ought to love one another."* 1 John 2:7-11 reads," *Dear friends, I am not writing you a new command but an old one, which you have had since the beginning. This old command is the message you have heard. Yet I am writing you a new command; its truth is seen in him and in you, because the darkness is passing, and the true light is already shining. Anyone who claims to be in the light but hates a brother or sister is still in the darkness. Anyone who loves their brother and sister lives in the light, and there is nothing in them to make them stumble. But anyone who hates a brother or sister is in the darkness and walks around in the darkness. They do not know where they are going, because the darkness has blinded them."*

Oh friend, this is it! If we claim to be brothers and sisters in Christ but we are still acting hatefully towards each other, The Word says we are still walking in darkness. We're being blinded by our darkness and not allowing God's Light and love to provide what we need to love correctly.

I have no problem saying if you are still struggling with bigotry or hatred of any kind, you have yet to accept the full love God has for you, and you are still walking in some darkness. You need the blinding light of God's love and discipline and correction to heal you so you can learn to love correctly and stop hating.

This says if you hate a brother, you are still walking in darkness. This is huge. If you are harboring grudges, feuds and generational junk, please allow me to say to you, right now, you need to repent and get free immediately, or you cannot truthfully walk in the love God is calling you to walk in with Him.

You have an anointing to protect as well. 1 John 2:20-27 says, *"But you have an anointing from the Holy One, and all of you know the truth. I do not write to you because you do not know the truth, but because you do know it and because no lie comes from the truth. Who is the liar? It is whoever denies that Jesus is the Christ. Such a person is the antichrist—denying the Father and the Son. No one who denies the Son has the Father; whoever acknowledges the Son has the Father also. As for you, see that what you have heard from the beginning remains in you. If it does, you also will remain in the Son and in the Father. And this is what he promised us—eternal life. I am writing these things to you about those who are trying to lead you astray. As for you, the anointing you received from him remains in you, and you do not need anyone to teach you. But as his anointing teaches you about all things and as that anointing is real, not counterfeit—just as it has taught you, remain in him."*

You and I need to protect our anointing, and our great commission God has given us to go into the whole world and preach the gospel. We protect it by remaining in Him.

Remaining in The Love God has for us protects us from losing our effectiveness in the
Kingdom. Remaining in God's love allows us to love correctly.
Remaining means staying.
Remain in Him.
Abide in Him.
Live in Him.
Stay completely attached to Him.

When we abide in the Vine or remain in the Vine, we can love correctly. We must stay attached to Jesus to love like Jesus. We can't do it without Him. Without Him we are swayed by our feelings. We believe lies easily. We let our flesh rise and rule. We get offended. We get into unforgiveness. We say mean things, do mean things and forget to show compassion. We must stay attached to the Vine Jesus Christ to be the loving vessels God is calling us to be.

"I am the true vine, and my Father is the gardener. He cuts off every branch in me that bears no fruit, while every branch that does bear fruit, he prunes so that it will be even more fruitful. You are already clean because of the word I have spoken to you. Remain in me, as I also remain in you. No branch can bear fruit by itself; it must remain in the vine. Neither can you bear fruit unless you remain in me. "I am the vine; you are the branches. If you remain in me and I in you, you will bear much fruit; apart from me you can do nothing. If you do not remain in me, you are like a branch that is thrown away and withers; such branches are picked up, thrown into the fire and burned. If you remain in me and my words remain in you, ask whatever you wish, and it will be done for you. This is to my Father's glory, that you bear much fruit, showing yourselves to be my disciples. "As the Father has loved me, so have I loved you. Now remain in my love. If you keep my commands, you will remain in my love, just as I have kept my Father's commands and remain in his love. I have told you this so that my joy may be in you and that your joy may be complete. My command is this: Love each other as I have loved you. Greater love has no one than this: to lay down one's life for one's friends."
John 15:1-13 NIV

Jesus commands us to love each other. How are we doing with that? Does He say, *"My command is, love those that agree with you?"* Or *"Love those that are the same political party as you?"* Or *"Love those that are the same culture or color as you?"* No, He says love each other, period! And, unless we remain in the Vine, we will drop the ball loving correctly every day and twice on Sundays

We are called to lay down our lives for our friends. Does that mean literally all the time? No. But we do need to lay down our agendas and our schedules sometimes for friends. Lay down our checkbooks sometimes for our friends. Lay down our opinions sometimes for our friends. Jesus laid down His life for us. Do you think we could lay down our posting on social media sometimes? Maybe, thinking twice before we text back a mean text, or post a passive aggressive post.

1 John 3:16-19, *"This is how we know what love is: Jesus Christ laid down his life for us. And we ought to lay down our lives for our brothers and sisters. If anyone has material possessions and sees a brother or sister in need but has no pity on them, how can the love of God be in that person? Dear children, let us not love with words or speech but with actions and in truth. This is how we know that*

*we belong to the truth and how we set our hearts
at rest in his presence."*
Oh friend, it's about loving correctly. Loving God
and loving people correctly.

Loving requires sacrifice. We don't do good works
and sacrifice to make ourselves feel good that
we've done our good deed of the day. We love
because He first loved us. We love and give
because there are people in need, and we have
material things that can help them. We give
because of God's love, and we give to show God's
love. We don't give to get God's love. He already
loves us and there's nothing we can do to get God
to love us more and nothing we can do to get Him
to love us less. He is that Prodigal Son's Father who
just wants to love us no matter what.

The Word says we don't love just with words, but
with actions. That's how the world sees something
different in us and wants what we have. Our love
and our compassion and our sacrifice draw people
to truth, not fear. Fear has to do with punishment.
Perfect Love casts out fear and perfect Love draws
people to Jesus.

I sometimes think of outreach and loving people to
Jesus like the old movie ET when Elliot uses Resees
Pieces to get ET to come out to meet him. He lures

him out with candy then he shows him he wants to love him. We need to use love and outreach to lead people to their true Love Jesus Christ.

Our Unforsaken Women's ministry food pantry feeds thousands of hungry people each year. But we don't just feed people to keep their bellies full. We feed them to love them then show them Jesus' love for them is the bread of life that will never run out.

Our resale shop helps fund the ministry, but we don't just sell merchandise to help pay single moms and widows bills and sponsor enrichment scholarships for these families or help keep them from homelessness; we do these things for them to show Christ's love and to share Jesus with them so they will truly heal and be made whole to go to Heaven someday.

Our store and ministry volunteers don't show up every day just to "feel good" about themselves because of their charity work. They serve week after week, year after year at this ministry, to make a difference in the Kingdom of God and to make sure Heaven is crowded someday because Jesus became their Lord.

We haven't done Unforsaken Women's worship events each month for almost 14 years now because we like to have a girl's night out. We show up month after month year after year, because each seat in the worship center represents a soul. Every woman that attends have minds that need to be renewed in The Word of God.

Love is a verb. We don't just love with words or speech but in action and truth. Our outreaches that we do in ministry are the catalyst of love God's people, used to help restore hope to those who are hurting, and to help them find out they are unforsaken, and that God will never leave them and never forsake them.

Love draws people to the truth.
Love draws people to good decisions.
Love draws people to dignity.
Love draws people to hope.
Love draws people to Jesus.

When Mom Dies

August was one year since my Mama went to be with The Lord. I can say most assuredly she is with The Lord. She loved Jesus and her life showed it. My Mama fought Rheumatoid arthritis for almost 40 years. 40 years of flare ups and medications, some that worked, many that didn't. 40 years of pain and hospital visits and a slow, painful deterioration of her body frame. I went with my mom to some of her doctor's appointments and it never failed to amaze me how one 100-pound woman could handle what she handled.

She was a fighter in every sense of the word. She fought for her health. She fought to keep her marriage of 56 years healthy, and she fought in prayer and love for all her now 87 family members including her husband, kids, their spouses, grandkids and their spouses and her great grandkids.

She fought to keep Dad and all of us sitting in those pews at church whether we felt like it or not. She fought for Sunday dinners together and holidays celebrated together even if that meant meeting in the barn because their newest house wasn't done being built yet.

Her last Christmas here on Earth she filled 84 stockings. 3 great grands have been born since making our large family number 87. That's 87 family members with 95 percent of us living within 20 minutes of each other. What a blessing that is. I know. I count my blessings daily.

My Mom held our insanely big, close, family together. I'd love to say it was my mom and dad, but my Daddy would even say to you today, *"This family is as close as it is, because of your mother"*.

I can honestly say he is right. Since mom's passing, our family has felt the strain. We all love each other, don't get me wrong, but her absence has allowed much fleshly behavior to be tolerated that would never have been allowed when mom was here. Mom would have given us a firm "Knock it off." And, we would have shipped up, no matter what age, gender or position in the family was. She's not here now and we are all still trying to find our role in this family unit without her. Too real? Sorry, I don't know how to be any other way.

My Daddy is starting to get his smile back. I prayed and prayed for this for over a year now. He didn't really know how to live without her. He had only done that in the first 17 years of his life. His grieving has been a process and however he chooses to grieve is the right way. Everyone grieves differently.

Almost two years later he still drives to the cemetery daily to visit her, rain or shine. His love for her is so beautiful. It's truly a death till we part, sort of love.

He's a cowboy, who rode in the rodeo when he was young, and he built every house we have ever lived in with his bare hands. He broke horses and he hunts and fishes for much of his food. Though he is tough as nails physically, he raised us 7 kids with the softest demeanor and the heart of a shepherd. I think you can tell I've always been a Daddy's girl. My love for animals and the outdoors came from him.

But any bit of fight any of us have in us came from mom. She taught us to fight for what is right. That is a godly character most of the time, unless you are trying to win an argument. Which in that case, can be a liability. Mom and Dad taught us to stand up for what is right, no matter if anyone else is standing with you or not.

So, as we have been attempting to keep our family together and healthy without Mom here, there have been some knock down drag out fights, usually by text, which can be the most vicious.

We always make up quickly when we fight though. Mom taught us that too. I remember being young and fighting with siblings and we would say *"I hate you."* Then Mom with tears in her eyes would say, *"You never say hate to your brother or sisters."* She told us multiple times a story of her childhood and how she said she hated one of her sisters during one fight, and it was storming outside and a branch came through the window and almost hit her sister. She cried and asked God to forgive her and never said she hated anyone again. I'll never forget that story.

Siblings argue. Spouses argue. Families argue. The death of a loved one is only one trigger of these arguments. No family is perfect, and we all need grace and mercy and forgiveness. But we better learn to dish grace out liberally if we want it liberally. If we forget this, don't worry, the Word will remind us. *"Be kind and compassionate to one another, forgiving each other, just as in Christ God forgave you."* (Ephesians 4:32 NIV)

"Bear with each other and forgive one another if any of you has a grievance against someone.

Forgive as the Lord forgave you." (Colossians 3:13 NIV)

"For if you forgive other people when they sin against you, your heavenly Father will also forgive you." (Matthew 6:14 NIV)

Listen, I'm a grace giver because I'm a grace needer. I know needer isn't a word, but it makes good sense to me. The last time our sibling group text caused a little drama in the family it lasted about 24 hours. Then Holy Spirit convicted and corrected most of us and the apologies started flowing.

Personally, God put this little beauty from Romans on my heart until I humbled myself and asked for forgiveness for some mean words I had texted. *"Love must be sincere. Hate what is evil; cling to what is good. Be devoted to one another in love. Honor one another above yourselves. Never be lacking in zeal, but keep your spiritual fervor, serving the Lord. Be joyful in hope, patient in affliction, faithful in prayer. Share with the Lord's people who are in need. Practice hospitality. Bless those who persecute you; bless and do not curse. Rejoice with those who rejoice; mourn with those who mourn. Live in harmony with one another. Do not be proud but be willing to associate with*

people of low position. Do not be conceited. Do not repay anyone evil for evil. Be careful to do what is right in the eyes of everyone. If it is possible, as far as it depends on you, live at peace with everyone. Do not take revenge, my dear friends, but leave room for God's wrath, for it is written: "It is mine to avenge; I will repay," says the Lord. On the contrary: "If your enemy is hungry, feed him; if he is thirsty, give him something to drink. In doing this, you will heap burning coals on his head." Do not be overcome by evil but overcome evil with good."
Romans 12:9-21

What a friend we have in Jesus. What an honor to serve Him. What a blessing we have in His Word that cuts straight through joints and marrow and judges the thoughts and attitudes of the heart. When we hear God tell us to *"knock it off"* (like my Mama used to tell us when we were arguing), and we listen and obey, peace returns.

Truthfully, I am grateful to be part of a family that has healthy conflict resolutions. We don't always feel like apologizing, but we eventually crucify our flesh and do it anyways. It reminds me of my sweet niece who is now grown into a lovely lady. When she was about two or three and would have to sit in time out for being unkind in some way, when told to apologize, she would say, *"I can't like sorry.*" Her mother would say "*I know honey, I can't like it either, but Jesus gives us the strength to.*"

When mom passed away a huge void was left in our family. Truthfully, we have all worked hard in different ways with all of our different gifts and personalities to make good out of our new normal. She's missed dearly and we must keep reminding ourselves how happy she is in Heaven right now, and how happy we will be someday when we are reunited with her. That is the hope that is an anchor for our souls.

The transition from Mommy to Mimi has brought a realization of just how precious health, wellness and everyday life is. It's a gift to simply wake up each morning and have another day to say, "*This is the day that The Lord has made, we will rejoice and be glad in it.*"

A Menopause Minute

Well, I did it. I had a complete hysterectomy. Once again, Mo's plans were not God's plans. I have always imagined myself going through the change of life naturally, steadily, rocking in a rocking chair next to my husband, embracing the changes of life together. I have been rocking In a rocking chair, but for a few months, I've needed a cushion. I had major surgery 5 months ago.

I not only had my uterus out, but I also had a complete hysterectomy as my maternal grandmother had ovarian cancer and there was no need for me to deal with that later in life. I am officially in menopause. Though I thought my menopause story would be gradual and natural, God decided otherwise. I went into surgery with all my organs and hormones, I came out without them.

You can imagine this decision was not easy for me. I was scheduled for another appointment with my functional doctor who is mostly a naturalist. She has been working with me for four years now trying to get my excessive uterine bleeding to be under control, to regulate my hormones, and to keep me balanced, mind, body and soul. She's been such a blessing. I was calling her to set up my follow up appointment to go over my blood work results. She surprised me more than I can say when the words that came out of her mouth were, "Mo, I think you need a hysterectomy." I was shocked and in immediate tears as I truthfully had imagined my numbers were looking better. I guess I imagined it wrong.

I had been fighting anemia and irregular heavy bleeding for such a long time, she said she was concerned about my other organs aging too quickly because of it. She asked how I felt about it, and through tears I told her I trusted her, and I trusted my OBGYN who was actually suggesting the same thing. God had decided to finally make it clear to me. So, I called our friend who is my OBGYN and asked him to schedule my surgery. He moved a ton of things around at the office to make it happen as quickly as possible. He and my functional doctor both encouraged me that enough was enough. It was time for a change.

You know, that's how this old girl works? I need a kick in the overalls sometimes. I don't ever enjoy change. But God works so beautifully in change. I know this, but I just forget it so often.

To spare you all the recovery info. I'll just say, today as I lay in the bathtub reading a book and listening to instrumental worship music, I thanked God over and over for my health. I experienced a supernatural recovery from my surgery and the years and years of constant bleeding bouts that are officially over, in Jesus Name.

I was released from the hospital less than 28 hours after surgery. I went home to a comfortable sitting place on my porch in the sun to get extra vitamin D, a comfortable recliner in my family room where "When Calls The Heart" (from The Hallmark Channel) was binged in between naps and barefoot walks on the grass for grounding. I was cared for by a loving husband (who thank God can work from home often) and a mother-in-law who stayed by my side to make sure I followed the rules and didn't end up in the garden or barn, throwing hay bails too soon.

My college age son Eli was such a blessing to me, picking up my slack with dishes and laundry and housework while I couldn't do it. Truthfully, I love housework. It was hard for me not to do it. The first time I could vacuum and not feel any kind of pull of my skin, I felt so free.

I listened to the doctors' orders for once in my lifetime. I didn't push my recovery too fast as I was terrified of having to go back to the hospital because I had un-done something that was done well. I didn't lift too much, I didn't stretch too much, I didn't do any more than the paperwork suggested. I wanted this to be one and done. And God blessed that. God not only blessed that, but He also inspired the writing on the rest of this book. And I think my spiritual obedience has grown a bit. See, you can teach an old dog new tricks.

I'm beyond grateful that a lot of the side effects of a quick drop of hormones haven't affected me too much. I pay a lot of merit to the good herbs I take for my brain, theanine, ashwagandha and melatonin. I also take a handful of supplements in the morning as well as drink raw milk, eat fresh meat and eggs from our farm and vegetables from our garden. I am not on hormone therapy as of now, but if God calls for it, I have learned to never say never with The Lord. I do not like the spiritual spankings I have had to take over the years. So, if God says yes, I say yes. If God says no, I say no.

Truthfully, I could be getting hot flashes and not even know it, as I sweat a lot as a farmer. I could be dealing with mood swings but truthfully, as a minister and someone in full time ministry, I've dealt with spiritual warfare so long, I have learned how to crucify the ups and downs in my flesh and emotions and silence the talk of the enemy when he tries to get me riled up. Truthfully, I could be dealing with lack of sleep, but all day long I wear myself out so much working hard on the farm, watching grandbabies and in the ministry, I drop at night, whether hormones want it or not. The scripture is true, *"The sleep of a laborer is sweet."* Ecclesiastes 5:12

I am 5 months post-surgery and it feels great. I'm up to 45 crunches (ab work) a day and I walk about two miles 3 times a week. I lift light weights and I'm getting my strength back when doing chores. It feels so good. The human body is miraculous. When I think of all the organs that were taken out and all of the other ones in there having to find their new places, I'm amazed. God is so…. cool.

Modern medicine is so cool. I had robotic surgery. Robots and my doctors took me apart and put me back together and I lived to talk about it. When I was discharged from the hospital the day after the surgery, I told my doctor I didn't want any pain medication. I said, *"I'll take ibuprofen."* I didn't want to deal with any of the side effects of narcotics. He respected my decision. At my follow up appointment 6 weeks later, I was given a clean bill of health. He said, *"Mo, you are a tough cookie, you handled major surgery with over-the-counter medication."* My inner cowgirl felt so good.

God is good. He is faithful and loving and when He needs to put His foot down so we listen, He will. He is our Daddy, and we need to trust that He has our best interests at heart. I will always trust that no matter what He calls me to. If God calls you to do something. He will see you through it. He's with us. He goes before us. He's in us. He will never leave us, never forsake us. We are Unforsaken.

The Playhouse

We turned our pool shed into a playhouse for our grandkids for Christmas this year. We also had my dad build a silo with a slide coming out of the front of it and we attached it to the side of the playhouse.

The shed was easy to keep shut as we renovated it without them figuring anything out, but the silo construction had to be quick and strategic to keep the kids surprised as my grands are usually here at the farm at least once or twice a week.

Christmas morning with the family was magical. I don't know who loved it more, our adult kids and their spouses or our grands. Our whole family had matching Christmas pajamas on as we spent hours sliding down the slide and playing house, grocery store and dress up. It was truly a hit, and it has been since.

The truth is this whole farm has been one building project or one animal purchase at a time with my kids and grandchildren's hearts in mind. When we think of something that would make them want to be here more, we work our hearts out to make those ideas and plans a reality. Why? Because my tribe is my hobby. Jesus and my family are my life. My people are my everything.

I'm dedicated to making this 5-acre farmhouse that we bought, into a fully functioning regenerative farm. I'm serious about taking this land that was abused by neglect, fertilizer and chemicals, into a place where every living organism and microorganism can survive and thrive here, in a way that honors God's original design of allowing the animals and the plants to live and move and live their lives being on the land, and at the same time helping to build and support.

I was amazed when we looked at this land that there was only one, lone, palm tree on the whole property. Being a lover of gardens and trees and nature, I think, the desire to take an empty canvas and fill it with life, excited me the most.

Every plant that is on this land was planted by us. Every outbuilding on this land was built or bought and brought here by us. Every animal that lives here was hand-picked and cared for by us. Please excuse me as I clarify. When I say us, I mean, God, Tommy and me, (with a lot of help from my dad and my son Eli.)

We have cows, chickens, goats and pigs, as well as our amazing border collie Hady who makes this whole dream work. Each animal provides for this land or home in one way or another, whether through meat, milk, eggs, or even pooping, to provide the most amazing fertilizer you could ask for in the garden.

I've learned so much over the past four years living here and I have so much more to learn. We have so many more ideas of what we want to do here and it's so much fun learning as we go. Farming is truly amazing and can only have been created by the Master Farmer Himself, God.

The truth is, Tommy and I do not work hard on this homestead to build our dream farm, that doesn't motivate us at all. This farm is not for us. We work for God. We work to give good gifts to our tribe, our kids and their spouses, our grands and future grands and great grands. We learned it from our God. Matthew 7:11 says," *If you, then, though you are evil, know how to give good gifts to your children, how much more will your Father in heaven give good gifts to those who ask him!*"

Everything I do, I do with legacy in mind. What will Tommy and I leave behind? What will live past us? I think of this with every book I write. I don't write to make money. That even made me giggle as I typed it. I don't even make a dime on my books. I endowed all my royalties to the ministry. I write books to help people now and I write books to help people in the future. I want my writing to live past me. With the ministry owning them, that is guaranteed.

God's Word is the same yesterday, today and forevermore, so it excites me to think of someone reading one of my books and finding hope in Jesus 150 years from now. Why not? I write with legacy in mind.

Everything we do on this homestead is with legacy in mind. We changed the pool shed into a playhouse. Why? Because I want my tribe to come here often, because I want to continue encouraging them in The Lord as often as I can. I'm not a good, once a month visit, kind of Mama or Mimi. I'm obsessed with my people, and I'm obsessed with them knowing it. We built the playhouse for them, because they are important to us. Jesus and my family are my life. My people are everything to me.

You Can Always Paint the Silo

It seems like I always have paint on my hands. I'm never going to be asked to be a hand model. Whatever oil based or water-based color that is on my hands at any one time can pretty much clue you into what I have been occupying my afternoon coffee boost of energy with that day.

Right now, I'm typing with white speckles on my hands. I've been touching up paint for about an hour. It started with a simple cereal bowl of paint and a brush; to touch up a couple shadows that were coming through on the silo slide we built the kids.

As I was standing at the silo, in the sun, by the pasture behind me, all I could hear was the whistling of birds and the slight movement in the brush behind me from perhaps bunnies or squirrels. It was heavenly standing there stroking the brush up and down. I thought how badly I needed that peace and quiet. It's been a busy season lately.

As I was painting, I thanked God for purpose. There is something about painting that always makes me think of purpose in life. After all, paint will always have to be touched up somewhere here at the farm. Whether it's the black, x-rail fence that chips off from the Florida sun, or the white paint on the shed, the house, chicken coop, staircases, or patio. And that's just outside of the house.

After I brushed the spots that I had seen needed it, I moved around the bottom of the shed, then took that white paint in to touch up my fireplace because by the end of the winter, the block gets dingy from soot, so I must scrub it, and touch up the white paint. Most people would probably not do this yearly. But this girl is enamored with a fresh, clean, painted look. I moved from the fireplace to the baseboard in the kitchen and under my cabinets. This took me about an hour all together.

Why am I sharing my afternoon chore list with you? Because, as I was thanking God for purpose I thought about housewives and mothers and wives. I thought about my sister's joke that laundry is job security for her. It will never end.

I thought about how purposeful we can be, caring for our homes and families and what a blessing that can be. It doesn't always feel that way, does it? The devil loves to get in your head as a homemaker and tells you how unimportant your days are. I can hear his lies right now, like, *"How many times can you unload and load the dishwasher and wipe the same counters? Isn't there something exciting you would rather be doing? Don't you have any dreams? You know you could have been an actress. What if you married that man from high school? Your life would be so much more fun right now. But instead, you're wiping noses and washing socks that you'll never find the right match for."* Oh, the devil is a liar.

My friend, the never-ending chore lists at our house aren't burdens, they are opportunities. Chores are opportunities to glorify God in our work. Work is a gift from God, no matter how hard or simple it is. How we respond to that to-do list is what matters.

Colossians 3:17 says, *"And whatever you do, whether in word or deed, do it all in the name of the Lord Jesus, giving thanks to God the Father through him."* We are to do everything to glorify God.

When Tommy and I scoop poop out at the barn, I'm glorifying God by taking good care of my animals and land and building a compost pile that is good for my garden. When I bake my sourdough bread, I am glorifying God by caring for our family's health and our bodies which are the temples of The Holy Spirit.

When I keep my home tidy, I am respecting the gift of a home that God gave me so that He sees how grateful I am for that gift. When we cook meals for friends and family and invite them to eat with us, we offer hospitality and love for others in friendship.

When we are vacuuming, dusting, mopping, cooking, cleaning the fridge, organizing the garage, or cleaning out the car, we are remembering that everything we own belongs to God and we are called to manage those gifts well.

There's always a silo to paint. There are always floorboards that could be wiped. There's always laundry to do. How about we change how we feel about that by thanking God for purpose? Purpose keeps us alive. I truly believe that. When you take purpose away from people, they can lose hope and hope deferred makes the heart sick.

So, today, Mama, as you undertake your chore list, take a minute to thank God for the health you have, to do hard work, a body that works, and a mind that is sharp and can see His hand in everything. God truly meant it when He wrote in Ecclesiastes 3:12-13. *"I know that there is nothing better for people than to be happy and to do good while they live. That each of them may eat and*

drink and find satisfaction in all their toil—this is the gift of God."
I'm so thankful for the silo to paint.

Boundaries

If I've learned anything from farming it is, to shut
the gate. When heading out to the pasture or barn
for anything you had better be quick on the draw
with grabbing the gate behind you. If not, you
could be chasing livestock away from your
perfectly, ready to harvest lettuce crops.
Those animals are quick and smart, especially my
goats.

 One of the first things we did when we bought this
land was to hire a fence company to come and put
up hog fence. Our entire house and pasture are
fenced for the protection and livelihood of our
animals, and the garden. Now that I have
grandbabies, those fences and our automatic gate
are a lifesaver.

We are great at creating boundaries for our
animals, our land, and our homes. But, how about
our lives? How good are we at setting limits with
people and letting them know the comfortable
amount of space and time that we need for
ourselves? I know I stink at it.

 I set boundaries and I do good keeping them for a
little while. Then, someone asks me to "just this
once" enlarge that boundary to include something

that they need. Then, before I know it that boundary is down, and people are trampling all over me like a stampede of cattle.

I love people and that is a necessary trait for a minister. The most important commandment is to love God and love people. But truthfully, that love I have for people can become a liability if I am not careful to protect myself from burn-out.

This New Years I set a resolution to have healthier boundaries for work in the ministry, work on the farm, work babysitting my grands, and work caring for my home and family. How am I doing? Well, I am doing better than I thought I would be doing. But it is only February.

I set a color-coded calendar to help me keep my time organized. Purple represents time with God, studying His Word, ministry and church activities. Red represents farm time and housework. Green represents time resting and taking care of myself physically. And blue represents babysitting time. I knew the blue ones would be my hardest boundaries to keep as I have a hard time saying no to the kids and grands. I love being with them very much.

I sent the calendar to the kids to let them know what days they could count on me for babysitting.

They all put a heart on the screenshot I had texted them and within minutes, I had two requests for that Friday night babysitting so they could have date nights. I told them both yes and said we could have a cousin's night here at the farm. I told Tommy that we were booked for Friday.

It was about two days into my schedule when one of the kids *"jokingly, but not jokingly"* asked, *"So, how set in stone are your "No Saturdays?"* To say this could have been the quickest broken New Year's resolution in history would be an understatement. I held my ground though. Thank you, Jesus.

Truthfully, I was giggling with God yesterday morning. During my prayer time I said to Him, "God, we are pretty much running a toddler Airbnb here at the farm." Quite honestly, my kids and their spouses aren't afraid to ask for early drop off and late pick up either.

When the family is here and after we have eaten dinner, they will bath those babies in the tub and just shoot those little dirty clothes down the laundry chute, as if to say, *"housekeeping will do it."*

They aren't afraid to ask for the hot tub or pool to be turned up to warm, comfortable temperatures so that the kids can swim year-round to keep up their swimming lessons skills. Papa and Mimi's answer is a resounding, *"No problem, of course."* There are always vanilla and chocolate cookies in the cupboard, every kind of weird milk Pinterest has decided trumps cows' milk now for kids, and juice boxes by the case, ready and chilled to their liking. Sunday cones are always in the freezer, or occasional Mickey Mouse ice cream cones if there is a sale.

Each time they leave, I sanitize all toys, so as not to spread the winter boogers all around, and restore the farm and playhouse to neat, tidy and up to my OCD standards.

I truthfully can't lay off any new, fun, farm animal toys that come into our thrift shop from time to time and I'm a sucker for a John Deere tractor toy. So, when the kids leave and I hear the question, *"Mimi, can I take this home?"* My answer is most assuredly, *"Sure, my love."*

I have every kind of diaper here in case they forget them. I have extra jammies in case they spend the night. We even purchased our own baby monitor camera to keep an eye on them as they sleep.

We have bikes, scooters, sidewalk chalk and bubbles, kites and balls to meet their every need.

All of which I've purchased from our thrift shop of course. That always eases my spending guilt as I feel it's also blessing the ministry, so it's a win-win.

We try hard to make sure we base the new animal babies that we get here on the farm around holiday gifts the kids will love. For example, baby chicks or bunnies at Easter time and baby pigs at Christmas. I think this year will be bunnies. I can't wait.

Oh, and I also catch every cold and virus they get. Why? Because boogers or not, if they lean in for a hug or kiss, this Mimi will be right there to squeeze them tight. I laugh when I think of what a germaphobe I was a couple years ago before the grandbabies came along. Not anymore. I'm a walking antibody now, like a pediatric nurse or schoolteacher. I'm in it! You name the childhood winter virus, and those loves of mine have shared it with their Mimi. I keep the vitamin store in business.

So, when you ask, how am I doing with those boundaries? Well, for ministry, and farm work, and my exercising work, I'm killing it. I'm staying right on target. I say no when it's not something I can do, and I don't feel bad about it, and I work hard at keeping my commitment no matter how big or small. My word is my bond.

Then, where the kids and grands are concerned, I guess I would say, I'm doing horrible. I can't say no to them. I can't even try. I'm obsessed with them, and so is Tommy. We are definitely overworked, understaffed and burning the candle at both ends.

Some sunset nights when we are juggling three two-year-olds on to the golf cart and driving them out to the barn with their cute little barn boots on, to feed the animals before bed, we look at each other and say, *"They won't be 2 forever."* Maybe we will set some more boundaries next year.

Following

Someone asked me if I was following some Hollywood trial that was being televised and making a lot of headlines. I am not good at remembering names of movie stars or musical icons, so I had no idea what she was talking about.

The truth is, I follow goats into the barn to get their hay and I follow my border collie around the yard for our two mile walk each day. I sure enough follow enough two-year-olds around the house trying to get them to pee on the potty instead of hiding to poop. I do a lot of following, but not a lot of following rich and famous people.

Truthfully, I'm not a good follower of people at all. I have always been a leader. I don't like anything trendy. It feels like copying to me. I like to be unique and do new things and try new things and take a lot of Godly risks and trust God with the consequences. I feel a little like the old Barbara Mandrell song, *"I Was Country, When Country Wasn't Cool."*

The only following that I will always do is following Jesus Christ. I will follow Jesus anywhere He leads me. That sentence is scary to type, and one that I have hit backspace on so many times in my life, to hedge my bets that He will never send me to a third world country or to a cold climate again. But, this time, I don't know if I have just had too much diet cola and I'm feeling a little edgy, but I typed it, and I'll type it again. I will follow Jesus Christ anywhere He leads me.

I used to say this, but with guardrails up. Now, as a Mimi, not just a Mommy, I put it right out there, naked and exposed. I am not afraid to follow Jesus anywhere He leads me, because I know, if He leads me to it, He will be with me in it. I won't be alone, ever. I am Unforsaken. And that's a surefire guarantee for me of success.

Following Jesus doesn't mean success in the way the world describes it, but it is success in reaching the lost for Jesus. Success in God's terms means fruitfulness. To be fruitful for God means you will shine in dark places, look different than the world looks and people will eventually want what you have, not stuff, but peace.

Truly following Jesus will require hard work. I have never seen many Christ followers handed fruitfulness on a silver platter. It takes blood, sweat and tears crying out to The Wonderful Counselor over and over for help. Fruitfulness for God requires sacrifice, sacrifice of time, resources, and natural talents.

Following Jesus isn't a guarantee of a stress-free life. But it is a guarantee that when you encounter stress, you have a person to hand it to so that you can maintain your peace.

1 Peter 5:7 says, *"Cast all your anxiety on him because he cares for you."* To follow Jesus is to follow a caring leader Who wants to carry our burdens. I have not encountered that following any human. Most human leaders I have met want you to follow them, as you carry their baggage as well as yours.

Following Jesus isn't a get rich quick scheme, a get out of the hospital or jail free card, or a guarantee of long life. Following Jesus has only two promises attached to it; His presence and eternal life, and those two promises are more than enough. Jesus is enough for me. That's how I can say, I'll follow Him wherever He leads.

Following Jesus is exciting. I truthfully never know what each morning's coffee talk with Him is going to bring about. It may be God telling me to visit someone in the hospital who I saw reaching out on Facebook asking for prayer. It may be God telling me to invite the kids for dinner on Sunday and cook them spaghetti sauce. My morning talk with God could lead to Him showing me my next book idea or a business venture we could start with the ministry to raise funds to build affordable housing for single mothers and their children.

God may tell me to give my truck to someone who needs it, invite my dad over for breakfast or start a Bible study with my sisters. Following Jesus is exciting and fresh and full of surprises. It's never boring.

Do I always hear God right? Nope! Sometimes I have ideas that I thought God gave me, but it was just Mo. Sometimes I get ahead of God and start getting to work on ideas He has given me without doing the due diligence needed first.

Sometimes I share too much and teach things publicly that I thought was for the masses but was just for me. Do I mess up? Oh, heck yes. But thank God I serve The God of The Second and Third and Billionth Chances.

I love following Jesus. I have loved following Him since I was a young Mommy. I found Jesus as a young mom of a five-year-old and a three-year-old and I was ridden with anxiety, insecurity, guilt, shame, fear, and seasonal depression.

He saved a wretched soul when He saved me. I was a hot mess. I still am. I'm just a hot, forgiven mess, saved, redeemed, justified, sanctified and madly in love with The Savior of My Soul.

I am now a Mimi who loves following Jesus. I follow a God Who helps me daily to be an overcomer of anxiety, insecurity, guilt, shame, fear and seasonal depression. I am not an overcamer, I'm an overcomer. I work with Him daily to follow Him and His Word into the peace that passes all understanding.

It's the most amazing journey I've ever taken from Mommy to Mimi. One I thank God for everyday and will until I see Him face to face in eternity.

If you'll excuse me, I have to close now, I have some work to do. My kids and grands are coming for dinner tonight. I better batten down the hatches and thaw out some meat.

Made in United States
Orlando, FL
20 March 2025

59650771R00090